A Primer for Servant Leadership

ISBN: 1-4392-3538-4
ISBN-13: 9781439235386

To order additional copies, please contact us.
BookSurge
www.booksurge.com
1-866-308-6235
orders@booksurge.com

A Primer for Servant Leadership

Leading in the Right Direction

Dr. Howard L. Young

2009

CONTENTS

ACKNOWLEDGEMENTS

I am in deep appreciation of my wife, Barbara, who has through the years allowed me to pursue professional and academic pathways that have brought a deep sense of meaning to my life. Her encouragement has always been an essential part of the formula of any small successes I have known. Her love has sustained me for over forty years.

PREFACE

The book you now hold in your hand safely sat in my library for four years as a doctoral project, although I was strongly encouraged to submit it for publication when the manuscript was first completed in 2002. I have chosen to bring it off the shelf believing this work can help those presently leading institutions with a servant's heart or those who want to know more about this marvelous and incomparable way to lead others.

The manuscript remains in its original doctoral form for two important reasons. First, no tinkering with the basic text was needed in order for this book to fulfill the purpose of educating the reader to basic tenants and principles of Servant-Leadership. The text speaks succinctly and clearly to the nature and issues of servant-leadership. Furthermore, the final chapters of the text constitute a study for the application of "servant-leadership strategies" in selected churches in North Dakota and Montana. All pertinent materials and action-steps used within the text offer a template for those wanting to implement servant strategies within their particular institutions. Therefore, I am hopeful that readers recognize the adaptability of my simple strategies for their institutions, sacred or secular.

As a doctoral text, *A Primer for Servant Leadership* naturally borrows heavily from the thoughts of others. Some of the finest leaders and writers of our times provide rich and enduring servant-leadership thought as an integral part of this brief text. Hopefully, those writers quoted and recognized in this text will lead the reader into further exploration of the fascinating study of a powerful and effective way to lead others.

Dr. Howard Young

Chapter 1
LEADERSHIP CHALLENGES OF THE 21ST CENTURY

Leadership is always an issue in the Christian church. The ability of the Church to rise to any challenge lies largely in the ability of its leaders to lead. Research points clearly to the fact that effective leadership plays a primary and indispensable role in the church's ability to effectively respond to the environment around it.

George Barna acknowledges that while the burdens of criticism, loneliness, and the pressures that accompany leadership are deterrents that discourage individuals from accepting leadership roles in the church, the need to put more parishioners in critical leadership roles is a key to the church's future survival. Barna contends that while most churches have about 4 percent of their active adults in leadership, the number needed to successfully move churches forward lies somewhere between 8 to 12 percent. Barna's position is clear: a church cannot have too few leaders and make progress.[1]

An important question arises from Barna's conclusions. This question addresses the Church's need to embrace an appropriate model for active leaders and those they train. Such a model must adequately serve the church's endeavors to advance within its prevailing cultural environments. Although a plethora of leadership strategies exists, the most effective model(s) will strategically assist churches in impacting the culture around them while at the same time serving the needs of those already embracing the faith.

Discovering an adequate approach to Christian leadership becomes more important when one considers the constant possibility (and probability) of the failure of leaders. Failures occur within a wide variety of poor leadership attitudes and behaviors. The past two decades have seen a large number of moral failures. Leaders may also show poor personal financial accountability and/or outright dishonesty in the fiscal operation of an institution. There are also those in leadership positions who simply do not have the ability to lead institutions either in times of abundance or in times of scarcity.

Today there is a fresh call to leadership accountability. Leaders are under a mandate to lead not only effectively from an organizational point of view, but also in a manner that highly regards the prevailing spiritual, physical, and psychological needs of those being led. Consequently, leadership is not merely a pragmatic issue with effectiveness as the final criterion, but the spiritual side of wise, helpful, and nurturing leadership also comes into focus. Worldly models of leadership often fall short of this dual challenge to simultaneously serve the practical needs of the institution while at the same time serve the spiritual and life needs of those within the institution. This reality has led many back to the Scriptures where an enduring and invaluable leadership model may be discovered.

Humans Leading Humans

Christian leaders are fully human. They experience the full spectrum of human experience, feeling the impact and stress of their own humanity. Yet they are charged with the awesome task of leading other humans to levels of unselfish living that are extraordinary when compared to humankind's normal concept of conducting life. The problem lies in the leader's ability to manage his or her own humanness and then lead others beyond the dark side of their humanness. Such a formidable challenge calls for a new kind of leadership—a brand of leadership not commonly found in organizations controlled by traditional leadership thought or driven by popular opinions. This new kind of leadership is really an "old kind of leadership"—the leadership of a servant.

The ability to humbly lead as a servant does not come naturally or easily, even when the church experiences spiritual renewal. Even during high spiritual tides, the church may be hampered by centuries of entrenched thinking that encapsulates more from the worldly perspective than the heavenly one. Intense spirituality does not always translate into holiness or a more humble and serving lifestyle. The noble giftings of Christ to His church—prophecy, miracles, and other forms of divine intervention—can be trivialized and distorted in the service of self-aggrandizement and personal agendas. The atmosphere of triumphalism that often characterizes Pentecostal and charismatic fellowships can be counterproductive to attitudes of humility that lead to lovingly embracing the deepest needs of hurting individuals.[2]

Changing Times

The leader's own humanity compounded by the humanity of those he or she leads is only part of the problem. Rapidly changing social and economic conditions and cultural upheavals of various kinds mandate that leaders recognize the sociological factors influencing those being led. Leadership then proceeds to optimize every resource available to respond to the changes around them.

Good leadership assesses both the spiritual and sociological factors influencing those they lead and strategizes in a manner that rises to the occasion. Leaders who understand the forces of change on a culture and know how to adequately respond to these forces can transform a group of ordinary individuals into an extraordinary team that can make significant contributions to the environment around them.

The aspiring leader now arrives at a most difficult question: In what manner can a leader approach the overpowering issues created by a world driven largely by intemperance and cultural changes that erode Christian values? Wong rightly asserts that these overpowering issues demand a new and revolutionary kind of leadership. He calls it "*open leadership*". Wong believes the effective leader can unite a highly undisciplined and culturally variegated group of people, move them toward a common goal, and help empower them to move steadily toward its fulfillment. This is possible when traditional despotic leadership modes are forsaken and open leadership is practiced.[3]

Wong characterizes the open leader as one who regards an organization as a living organism designed for adaptive success, regardless of the social and cultural forces that seem to work against it. Furthermore, the open leader motivates the organism to move forward toward challenging goals and achieve the maturity and growth possible within a group of united individuals. His idea of leadership is revolutionary and suggests a great sense of openness.

> Open leadership goes beyond the notion of flattening the hierarchy; it calls for breaking down all structural barriers that hinder the exchange of creative ideas. It emphasizes functional leadership rather than positional leadership, such that any individual with the expertise to meet a certain demand will have the opportunity to exercise leadership.[4]

According to Wong, the key to open leadership as a viable model for tackling the toughest cultural and structural problems of leadership is its underlying connection with servant leadership.

Open leadership and servant leadership go together, because one cannot practice open leadership without having a servant's heart.[5] Providing a humane and spiritual face for the exercise of power, servant leadership calls the leader beyond his or her human experience and strikes a chord of compassionate and open interaction and exchange that is vital to success in the kingdom of God.

The pressure to have an enduring and relatively invulnerable leadership model in the church has led to a renewed interest in what Scripture teaches about leadership. Particularly, there has been a revived interest in what is commonly called "servant leadership." The idea of servant leadership has a secular and religious track, both of which are experiencing considerable development as the model is applied in the corporate and church worlds. As Horvath observes, whether secular leaders realize it or not, many corporate CEOs have introduced one of Christianity's major precepts into their corporate environments. Servant leadership has been increasingly acknowledged as the way to do business in the upcoming decades.[6] More important, the relative popularity of the servant-leadership concept has given rise to a rather aggressive treatment of the topic in current literature, prompting many leaders to thoughtfully and prayerfully reflect on the implications of an enthusiastically applied servant-leadership model within the church. At the same time it is ironic that secular organizations appear to be giving more credence to this biblical model of leadership than does the church for which this effective pattern of leadership was established!

This project reflects the imperative for the church to return to the biblical model of the servant leader. While there is an apparent yearning for the church to return to a Christ-centered rather than human-centered model of leadership, the response of current church leadership to the servant model demands more than mere sentimentality toward the scriptural model. There is a need for the correlation between what we profess as the ideal

Christian principles of leadership and the manner in which leadership is carried out within the church. Christ-centered leadership must be shorn up with Christ-centered living. The mandate to both live and lead in the Spirit of Christ is the core issue. As in so many other times of historical crises for the church, it is a time to return to the basics—those attitudes and practices of faith and humble living that give faith its marvelous attraction to outsiders and ministers compassionately to insiders.[7] In the words of the apostle Paul to the church at Philippi, the call is to imitate Christ's humility:

> Do nothing out of selfish ambition or vain conceit, but in humility consider others better than yourselves. Each of you should look not only to your own interests, but also to the interests of others. Your attitude should be the same as that of Christ Jesus: Who, being in very nature God, did not consider equality with God something to be grasped, but made himself nothing, taking the very nature of a servant, being made in human likeness.[8]

Recapturing the serving Spirit of Jesus remains a constant challenge to a church tempted to narcissistic behaviors and popular theology. Contemporary Christian leaders may need to readjust their thinking to a model of leadership that has as its roots the clear biblical teaching of the servant leader. Some have suggested that Moses was the first to practice servant leadership (Exod. 32:11-14, 30-35). Other Old Testament models of the servant leader include Joseph, Samuel, and Esther. It was in Jesus that servant leadership blossomed as a model for all kingdom leaders. Jesus explained that the servant-leader model was a superior way to lead when compared to the hierarchical and domineering model of leadership well known to His disciples.

When James and John asked Jesus if He would grant them the privilege of ruling positions in His kingdom, the rest of the disciples, whose thinking may have run along similar lines, were incensed at the request. Jesus used this awkward moment as an opportunity to explain that a philosophy of leadership so closely akin to that of the world was simply not acceptable in His kingdom. The idea of "great men" was simply incongruent with the leadership style He expected. "Whoever would be first among you must be the servant of all," He explained (Mark 10:44). Commenting on this incident, Page observes that the disciples were convinced that a certain type of power-wielding Messiah would restore the nation, but Jesus championed another style of leadership that drew suffering and struggling individuals into His kingdom. This kingdom would extol love and compassion as the daily standard of rule. The style that Jesus energetically supported was that of the servant leader.[9]

Survival of the Fittest

Does the Church's general abdication of the servant leader model have any relevance to its current challenge to survive in an ever-changing culture? The survival of the Church in the twenty-first century is a legitimate question in the minds of some current and well-known researchers. George Barna, founder and president of Barna Research Group, asserts that the contemporary church is incapable of responding to the present moral crisis in America. He calls for the reinvention of the church by the middle of this century, or face the frightening alternative of virtual oblivion of the Church within this century. According to Barna, current behavioral and lifestyle trends of American workers have filtered down into the relational and organizational dynamics of the church. While the American workplace is highly transient in nature, building a community of faith is by nature a focused and long-term proposition.[10] The lack of stability in the American workplace also finds expression in the inability of churches and their leaders to make long-term commitments and create enduring partnerships so vitally necessary for effective church ministry.

> Local churches find themselves always taking one step forward and two steps back because of the constant relearning curve and the loss of expertise brought about by continual departures of key players. If the church is going to maximize its influence, we must find ways to develop longer lasting commitments, both to relationships and ministry plans.[11]

The church's ability to fight decline lies in part in its ability to understand those forces that have put its back against the wall. The Presbyterian church, for example, lost 25 percent of its membership between 1965 and 1985, while other mainstream groups show comparable losses. A number of factors receiving the blame were church splits caused by music and style of worship, social and cultural upheavals of the past fifty years, a dramatic drop in birthrates in the past twenty years, and the unprecedented economic and geographic mobility that uproots one-fifth of the U.S. population annually.[12]

Additionally, the last decade has eroded the public perception of the Church's worth and relevance in life. A research report in the early nineties stated that most non-Christians indicated churches were not receptive or sensitive to their needs. Ninety-one percent of those polled indicated the church was not sensitive to daily needs while only 9 percent said churches were sensitive. During this same period of time, *Fortune* magazine surveyed churches and discovered that while 82 percent of the responding congregants believed their leadership felt deepening parishioners' spiritual lives was important, only 33 percent of those responding felt their pastors/leaders were very good at leading them into spiritual growth. Schaller calls this gap "the most important single factor" in the decline of traditional churches.[13]

The preceding observations must be matters of deep concern for those in church and pastoral leadership. A variety of thorny questions issue from these observations. What is the church's response to congregant perceptions that church leadership does not respond adequately to their need to develop more adequate spiritual lives? How can the church stay closer to the social and cultural forces that shape the attitudes of parishioners who expect the church and its message to stay relevant to both their personal and professional lives? How can the church escape the stigma of accusations that it has become narcissistic and self-serving? Is there any single factor that can respond to this collage of growing concerns? Given the complicated nature of pulling together the church as a unified community of faith and the unceasing cultural forces that insist on relevant and timely ministry that relates to both the pragmatic and spiritual needs of the individual, how can the church meaningfully respond to these pressing issues?

How Shall Christian Leaders Respond?

There is no single solution to the searching social, cultural, and relational issues facing the Church. There is, however, a primary response that takes into account the complexity of the relationships within church life and the outside forces that often confuse the church concerning issues of identity and mission. This response can be seen in the various attitudes, actions, and pastoral strategies flowing from church leadership that both advocates and practices a servant mentality. The passions of the servant leader will over time infuse with life the mission, vision, ministries, and programs of the church.

The Mandate of Servant Education

Key church leadership must view the multifaceted problems of the church ministering to the complex needs of a suffering planet as issues of education and training. If a significant part of the church's response to complexity and cultural change is compassionate and caring servanthood, then how shall Christian leaders train servants? Although it seems that methodical and serious training for servanthood and servant leadership would be a natural response for Christian leaders, the assumption of servant training can never be taken for granted. In fact, there is no guarantee that contemporary churches will take seriously the need to develop servants who can serve both churches and the cultures within which they exist. Brody argues that although the notion of "leaders as servants" goes back to the biblical days and perhaps even further, contemporary leaders seem to have forsaken this meaningful model in favor of leadership that focuses on self-aggrandizement and power.[14] If it is true that church leadership has largely followed the gurus of current leadership philosophies that either ignore or ridicule the values and practices of servant leadership, then it seems logical that the congregations of such leaders will unlikely be servants themselves. This danger compels the contemporary church to encourage its leaders to become servants themselves and then begin the important task of training their congregations in the simple truths and methods of the biblical servant.

Fundamentally, the challenge of training others in servanthood lies with key church leaders who understand the primary values that imbue the mission of biblical Christianity. They know a vital part of this mission is approaching both the church and the world with the servant attitude. A new birth of the servant attitude among leaders will compel them to examine the critical question of training servants and empowering them for the unique tasks facing the church today. Brody writes:

> The most effective servant leaders are usually great coaches and skill builders. Today the motto for productivity and competitiveness is 'ahead with the basics.' Don't lose track of the basics that got you where you are: your values system, beliefs, processes, and procedures. At the same time, have the courage to risk changing what doesn't work. Training may mean developing new or improved skills. Skills build confidence, and confidence builds skills; both are an essential part of the risk because each element reinforces and feeds the other.[15]

The simple approach of this project is itself a statement of response to the growing issues related to training servant leaders who can train others. If a training program focused on the call to servant leadership can result in meaningful and transformational strategies, what marvelous possibilities may present themselves when Christian leaders assume the responsibility of nurturing their churches in the principles of true servanthood!

It is hoped that the spirit and methodology of this project creates foundational thinking that can sustain long-term thinking that hardens into serious and protracted strategies that can over time transform a local congregation. There is no easy way for the church to enter the world of tangled and messy relations, personal failure, and pain. However, the mandate to build Christ's church was not based on an optimistic view of human nature or ideal cultural or social environments. Building Christ's church is not about favorable conditions; they will never exist. Moving the reign of God forward in the lives of hurting individuals requires the building of a caring community of people in the midst of challenging situations.

The church must be a house of caring servants, a community of people who find refuge in God and encourage one another to throw themselves on a merciful Savior. Servants are nurtured and grown against the forces of the time and cultural change. They come to learn that the only way to live in this world is to focus on the power of the spiritual life discovered in Christ. They live to share this life with the less fortunate who seem trampled by the world around them. Raising up servants for such challenges is never easy, but it is always worth it. The impact of the Church on the world is at stake.

Forward into Servanthood

Developing a training component to respond to the outstanding need to train servant leaders is a major goal of this study. The writer reasoned that training should be carried out in situations in which the value of servant leadership could be quickly appreciated. No places of true pastoral ministry are ever easy, but some present challenges more unique than others. Although any number of environments could respond well to the dynamics of this study, the writer chose the largely rural areas located in the states of North Dakota and Montana as focal points for the project. The rural demographic issues and lingering economic problems of these areas are well substantiated across the upper North Central Region of the United States. It appears that all major denominations are struggling to keep churches open and relevant in many rural communities, including churches within the Assemblies of God.

Challenges of the Assemblies of God

The North Dakota District is essentially a rural district of the Assemblies of God Fellowship. An interview with the district superintendent of North Dakota indicated deep concerns regarding his ability to provide pastors for a number of the district's rural churches. At the time of the interview, he indicated that approximately 10 percent of the district's churches needed pastors and at that point few viable candidates could be found for these rural situations. Pastoral terms in many rural areas of the state were usually quite short, lasting about three years on the average. Once a pastor left a church, it was not unusual for the church to take about one year to find a pastoral replacement.

Typically, pastors in these areas complained of small and ineffective congregations. There seemed to be little hope for numerical church growth in the hearts of the people and most parishioners were resigned to a virtual no-growth situation. The lack of social and economic amenities was also a drawback to long-term pastorates and deterrents for potential candidates. It seemed that most individuals looking for pastorates could not or would not resign themselves to the extreme rural conditions of the prairies and the rigorous winters of the northlands.

These are difficult situations that have lead to the closing of a number of churches in the Dakotas. The situation in Montana is not quite as desperate. It seems the overpowering natural beauty of Montana has a higher level of appeal, and the difficulty in recruiting new pastors to the area is not quite as defined as it is in the Dakota country. The superintendents from both districts did, however, indicate a strong desire to see more individuals committed to the small and difficult areas that need solid and committed men and women of God. Like many denominational leaders across America, these leaders were anxious about the future of their small, rural churches and were hopeful that a "revival of servanthood" could open more hearts to forgotten places of ministry. Furthermore, current pastors need a constant stream of hope and encouragement in these struggling rural areas, according to both superintendents. It is to this end that this project is dedicated. Biblical servants have a single standard for service: Life is given to please God. Geography and climate are secondary. While income and benefits remain important to those fulfilling ministry, it can be generally assumed that those going forth in a spirit of servanthood are more likely to accept the less attractive venues of ministry and simply trust the Lord to meet needs. The spirit of the servant must first ask, "What is your will, Lord?" All other questions and their answers have an adequate response through God's marvelous provision.

Chapter 2
SERVANT LEADERSHIP: BIBLICAL FOUNDATIONS

Servant Leadership and the Old Testament

From a biblical perspective, servanthood was the drama of dedicated individuals willingly performing a thousand unseen deeds of kindness without recognition. Biblical servants possessed an intuitive awareness that they were born not for themselves, but for others. Like many unseen virtues of the human spirit, servanthood existed within many biblical personalities, although their servanthood was not recognized as such or necessarily defined by words.

Although the New Testament would bring more definition to the role of servant leaders, particularly in the life of Jesus, the Old Testament is a bountiful resource for those who wish to discover the principal characteristics that are now commonly recognized as essential to effective servant leadership. Joseph, for example, had the opportunity to punish those who sought to harm him earlier in his life, but he chose to become their savior. Even though personal retribution would have seemed appropriate, forgiveness and service to his offending brothers was his deliberate choice (Gen. 45:1-14).

When Old Testament personalities demonstrated their relationship with Yahweh in terms of service and gave themselves in service to Him, they sometimes expressed servanthood to Him in a manner somewhat consistent with the culture around them.

Nevertheless, with the Hebrews, a new history for the term servant and its empowering concepts began.[16]

Moses was another early servant leader. Concerning Moses and the early patriarchs that preceded him, Bourbonnais observes:

> Strictly speaking, the biblical history of servant begins with Moses. The patriarchs no doubt had merited the title, servant of God, but it seems the ideas conveyed by the designation contained nothing original or specially marked, or they are later conceptions attributed to earlier times. When, therefore, Genesis names Abraham, Isaac, and Jacob servants of God, the frame of reference is borrowed from later writings or from notions that prevailed generally in patriarchal times. Already in Genesis, however, the idea of service evoked the idea of prostration, and this in turn suggests adoration.[17]

In the case of Moses, servant leadership often finds its most illustrious moments under appalling conditions. Although he was raised in Egyptian opulence, his heart would turn to his own people, the enslaved Israelites. An impulsive and misguided murder to his credit, Moses fled Egypt and opted for work in the desert. Forty years later, God pursued Moses in his retreat and isolation. Moses would go forward to serve Yahweh and lead His people.

Moses' leadership tasks with the enslaved nation began with the idea of service: "When you have *led* the people out of Egypt [says God], you shall *serve* Elohim on this mountain" (emphasis mine).[18]

Abad is here used as a classical term that speaks of service, or work in the service of someone. Following chapters in Exodus utilize significant terms which are consistently identified with service: *(abad)* service, *(zabaq)* sacrificing, and *(hagag)* celebrating a feast in honor of Yahweh.[19]

Under Moses' leadership, serving God was the equivalent of sealing one's faith by sacrifice, that would in turn bring Yahweh's presence, blessing, and protection. Moses' adventure in leadership—leading others into the service of God—would be a great, although difficult venture. Even when Israel rebelled against God, Moses rose to unselfishly lead his people. He could not imagine his continued existence apart from seeing divine benevolence and opportunity poured upon those he loved, in spite of the fact they flaunted their sins before a holy God. After seeing the unfaithfulness of his congregation firsthand, he returned to God with a prayer that only a servant of the people could pray: "Oh, what a great sin these people have committed! They have made themselves gods of gold. But now, please forgive their sin—but if not, blot me out of the book you have written."[20]

Samuel also exhibited the characteristics of a servant to the people. A unique leader even by biblical standards, Samuel filled the dual role of prophet and priest. He prayerfully and thoughtfully moved the nation through the transition from a theocracy to a monarchy. He dealt with a succession of incredibly difficult leadership challenges, but never lost his deep love for the people he endeavored to serve. In his parting speech that formally ended Israel's theocratic period, he pointedly asked about his personal habits and techniques as a leader. Considering the decadence of the times and the poor leadership immediately preceding Samuel, the peoples' answer is illuminating: "You have not cheated or oppressed us....You have not taken anything from anyone's hand."[21] Samuel maintained personal integrity and led with a high sense of responsibility toward his struggling people.

An appalling example of leadership that refused to serve the people and the consequences of arrogance and insensitivity in leadership was Rehoboam, the son-successor of Solomon. The elders of Judah instinctively recognized the foolish policies of their new young king, Rehoboam. In light of Solomon's disregard for the immense financial burden he placed upon those he led, the elders gave superlative advice to the new monarch, "Be a servant to the people and they will follow you," they challenged. But Rehoboam did not listen; he exacted more stressful policies upon his subjects and helped launch an incredibly dark period for his people.

One of Scripture's most noble stories of leadership is that of Esther. A rather bizarre series of events brought her to a strategic place in the Persian kingdom of Ahasuerus. The ability of a sovereign God to bring significant leaders to critical historical junctures should never be underestimated. At a time when a vicious plot could have derailed God's divine plan to restore His oppressed people and ultimately bring a Savior to the world, one woman stood between a nefarious enemy and God's beloved people.

The biblical record picks up Esther's story in the book that carries her name. The events of her life took place in the Persian Empire under Xerxes, approximately 475 b.c. Esther became a servant to her people, although she understood well the dreaded possibilities of going to the king unbidden. As a godly servant, she took a risk that was rewarded with kingly favor. The villainy of Haman was unmasked, Mordecai became a grand vizier, and her people were well prepared to defend themselves against the irreversible edict of the Persian king. Esther's sense of servanthood kept sacred history on track.

This sampling of Old Testament history provides an interesting cross study of several commonalities that existed among the servant leaders discussed. From a qualitative perspective, these leaders seemed naturally inclined to leadership. Making good decisions that favored oppressed and struggling people seemed almost natural for them. Providentially speaking, the good hand of God and what seemed to be their own natural leadership talent strategically positioned them in history's stream. They stepped forward on behalf of their people at critical, historical junctures. A sense of self-understanding and a deep love for those they led seemed wedded in their lives. Such qualities led them to a clear willingness to offer themselves in self-sacrifice for those who needed them. All of these individuals were servant leaders in embryo.

In all the preceding cases, these leaders stepped forward with a deep compassion for the people they led. Joseph's deep love for his brothers was not blunted by treachery, injustice, or years of separation from them (Gen. 45:4-14). His quick forgiveness of his offending brothers and salvific intervention for the family of Israel flowed as much from his personal compassion as from the historical circumstances of drought and hunger. Deeply caring for his oppressed people, Moses walked away from Egypt's comforts and compassionately chose identity with his own people (Heb. 11:24-26). Undoubtedly, Moses' strong identity with the enslaved Israelites was a significant component in his unique relationship with God (Exod. 32:30-32; 33:12-20). Samuel often experienced firsthand the moral weaknesses of the people he led, but he never failed to intervene for them at strategic times (1 Sam. 7:1-11). Furthermore, he tolerated their short sightedness (8:19-22) and led them with impeccable integrity (12:1-5). In a similar manner, Esther stepped into the flow of history and motivated by a deep concern for her own people, compassionately intervened at a crucial moment in Israel's history (Esther 5:1-8).

Courage was another common attribute of these early servant leaders. Joseph did not allow false accusations and unfair incarceration to blunt his God-given leadership abilities. He worked hard and remained faithful to God under terrible circumstances and over time emerged spiritually, morally, and emotionally intact, ready to lead and serve others again (Gen. 39:20-23). The histories recorded in Exodus, Numbers, Deuteronomy, and the writings of Samuel confirm that Moses and Samuel managed a number of spiritual and moral crises among those they led. Continuing courageously in the face of enormous odds, they served their people and brought them through oppressive circumstances. Esther summoned the courage to stand before her king and plead for the safety of her threatened people, an act of intervention that could have cost her life (Esther 7:3-5).

There was also a sense of the visionary within these Old Testament examples. Specifically, there seemed to be a visionary understanding of the long-term purpose of God for the people they served. Joseph knew that God had providentially placed him in Egyptian leadership for the purpose of preserving his family's posterity. Moses and Samuel served as interceding judges, and their acts, prayers, and guidance preserved God's people in dangerous times and secured their future. Esther knew that a calloused annihilation of her people could not serve the purposes of their destiny.

A Definition

The servant leader of the Old Testament was a unique combination of compassion that actively intervened for the safety, welfare, and preservation of others, courage that faced and conquered enormous odds, and a visionary sense that God had a continuing plan for those served. Old Testament personalities represent the fact that leaders were first servants of God and then, through compassionate, courageous, and visionary acts of leadership, became at the same time servants and leaders of the people. Often denying their own comfort and security, these leaders made themselves wholly available to those they led and served and depended upon resources beyond themselves, namely, the presence and strength of God.

Restoration and Blessing through the Suffering Servant

Isaiah, chapters 49-57, constitutes one of the most compelling sections of Old Testament literature. The previous nine-chapter section (chapters 40-48) focused primarily on Cyrus and his mission in Israel's restoration. The next section (chapters 49-57) points the reader to the Servant-Messiah who will restore the covenant people to their land before the coming of the Millennium. This unique section of Scripture is often divided into four parts: (1) The Servant turns to the Gentiles after rejection by His own people (chapters 49-50). (2) The believing remnant is blest and exalted (51:1-52:12). (3) The Servant will be shamefully abased but then deservingly exalted (52:13-53:12). (4) Salvation will be the gift of the Servant to both Jews and Gentiles in the Millennium (chapters 54-57).

The life and suffering of the Servant of the Lord is the powerful theme interwoven into Isaiah 52:13-53:12. This section of Isaiah introduces a radical idea to the messianic concept of the Old Testament, even one the disciples struggled to understand until after the resurrection of Christ.[22] Then they understood that Jesus merged the offices of reigning King and Suffering Servant.[23]

Whatever may be said about these sections of Isaiah, chapter 53 is to be understood in exclusively individual terms, fulfilled in Jesus, the Suffering Servant. It is readily understood that obedience to God's plan will always have a cost in the life of the Christian disciple or the Church as a whole. The atoning significance of the sufferings of the Servant, presented in chapter 53 are peculiar to Jesus, the unique servant.[24]

Filled with pathos and sorrow, Isaiah 53 is a graphic presentation of the Suffering Servant, capturing the death of the Servant and summarizing His vicarious suffering. It was He who was to bear the infirmities of suffering individuals and carry the sorrows for the accumulated sins of humanity. Isaiah's prophetic voice furnishes both foresight and insight into the nature and purpose of history's pivotal event: Jesus' substitutionary death on Calvary. Despised and rejected (verse 3), He will be pierced, crushed, punished, and afflicted with wounds (v. 5). The sacrificial offering of Jesus will be a source of both physical and spiritual healing.

The greater message of this marvelous chapter clearly relates to the complete work of spiritual redemption and healing provided by Jesus' death. That this is the main thrust of Isaiah 53 is clear from the words "transgression" (v. 5), "iniquities" (vv. 5, 11), "iniquity" (v. 6), "transgression" (v. 8), "wicked" (v. 9), "transgressors" [twice] (v. 12), and "sin" (v. 12). Sin and its horrible anguish are targeted and destroyed by the unspeakable gift of love from the Servant.[25]

There is no question that early Christians interpreted Isaiah 53 and other essential servant passages of Isaiah as a prophecy of Christ. The evidence for this is found in the New Testament (e.g., Acts 8:27-39; I Pet. 2:22-25).[26] According to Blocker, Jesus is clearly associated with the Servant Songs of Isaiah in the preaching of Peter.[27] Shortly after Pentecost, in the space of four chapters, Jesus is called the Servant four times (Acts 3:13, 26; 4:27, 30). Blocker notes this is evidence for some scholars that Christology—the doctrine of the person of Christ—was at that time primarily *paidology* (from *pais*, the Greek word for "servant").[28]

Isaiah 54 reflects the success and impact of the Servant's redemptive and sacrificial work. Developing the theme of growth, two vital comparisons are introduced. First, the "barren woman" is to sing and rejoice because the Servant's children are made hers. Paul applies this to the spiritual children of Jerusalem that are above (i.e., the New Jerusalem in heaven)—who are the spiritual (faith) children of Abraham.[29] A second comparison calls for enlarging "the place of the tent." The supernatural relationship implied in verses 1—3 culminates in the mandate to make room for the enlarging company of people who will come under blessings God has for His people because of the Servant's suffering, redemptive death, and resurrection.[30]

Leupold similarly sees the vital connection between the redemptive work of the Suffering Servant of Isaiah 53 and the successful Servant of Isaiah 54. This is an indication to him that Isaiah 54 is not a Servant Song that came as an insertion into the text at a later time, but a stirring affirmation that the blessings of Isaiah 54 holds and held its present position from the time of the first writing of the book. The promise to Zion of numerous offspring from the Servant's work (54:1-3) and an immediate reinforcement of that promise (vv. 4-10) would help the nation cast aside fear and confusion and accept hope for the future. The blessings of the Servant enable Zion to vanquish their fear (vv. 13-14) and neutralize any attack of the enemy (vv. 15-17).[31]

Isaiah's theme of servant would later appear in Paul's writing to the Philippians where Christ's obedience is a mark of servanthood (Phil. 2:5-11). Was Paul meditating on the Servant Songs of Isaiah when he wrote of Christ's humble death on the Cross, the pouring out of His life in service to others? Because He accepted the way of suffering, He has been exalted to supreme heights.

Isaiah's prophetic task was to take the understanding of Messiah as heir to David's throne to another level: Messiah as Servant of Jehovah. Isaiah painted a new picture of Messiah as Prophet and Priest by virtue of His suffering and self-sacrifice. The Savior of Israel and the Gentiles, executed by His own nation, but exalted by God to be both Priest and King, the Servant of Isaiah bequeaths a rich legacy to the Church of the future.[32]

Messiah as Servant of Jehovah is foundational to any serious inquiry concerning the nature of God Himself and how He carries out His work within His people. Isaiah does, in effect, confirm that God is a serving God, a missionary God who would ultimately find a full and compelling expression in the life, ministry, and sacrificial death of Jesus. Jesus' own words confirm this understanding of the essential nature of God and how His nature related to His visiting mankind: "For even the Son of Man came, not to be ministered unto but to minister, and to give His life a ransom for many."[33] Sent into this world by a loving God, Jesus understood His mission was not to receive ministry from others but to provide a serving ministry for others. This understanding of mission through service was at the core of His God-nature and eventually the ultimate expression of His life through sacrificial death.

Servanthood as expressed through Jesus was, therefore, less a leadership model than it was an expression of the very nature of God himself. Jesus' understanding of a missionary God visiting humankind through His ministry prompted Him to describe a flow of ministry that began with God, emerged in His own servant ministry, and continued through His disciples.[34]

Jesus' fulfillment of the roles as Suffering Servant and the Servant of Jehovah was a motivating example of love and witness for the church of the first century. That which the disciples saw in their Messiah was seen worthy of duplication in their own lives. As a Servant of God, Jesus impacted their future ministries and leadership through furnishing a redemptive life that personally transformed them and provided them with a compelling example of joy in the face of suffering, rejection, and misunderstanding that could inspire them in their own struggles. Indeed, they too would become suffering servants who led the Church in the crucial period of its early development. They did not fail in their tasks of leadership because they knew that leadership that flowed from a center of servanthood could flourish under the most difficult challenges.

The Messiah: Anointed to Serve

Jesus encapsulated every quality that constitutes the ultimate servant leader. His life reflected every attitude, behavior, and method that is now clearly seen as a preferred leadership model. Jesus' ministry captured the quintessence of servant leadership: a love for people that kept Him divinely intervening at the points of their individual struggles while at the same time empowering their most noble potential.

> The Spirit of the Lord is on me, because he has anointed me to preach good news to the poor. He has sent me to proclaim freedom for the prisoners, and recovery of sight for the blind, to release the oppressed, to proclaim the year of the Lord's favor.[35]

That which Jesus shared with His contemporaries finds its origins in Isaiah 61:1-2. Recalling that the Servant of the Lord was described as having the Spirit of God for doing His work (42:1), Isaiah 61 evidently picks up the servant theme and uniquely combines with it the corresponding theme of anointed Messiah. The Messiah from the line of David must have Spirit empowerment (1 Sam.16:14-23; 2 Sam.23:1-7; Zech. 7:12). The empowering Spirit is the strong taproot of His life and ministry and uniquely characterizes the only one to warrant bearing the name of the Christ—the truly anointed one. The term "anointed" appears in the text to indicate the distinct act of imparting the spirit of service and power, a commonly practiced procedure for those men inducted into office.[36] The activities prophesied by Isa. 61:1-2 were fulfilled in the anointed and sanctified life of Jesus. This anointing upon God's special Servant prevailed upon His human nature and earthly ministry throughout adulthood and never ceased until His final departure into heaven.[37]

Beyond His messianic anointing and empowerment, Jesus understood how those ennobled with the power to bring people into personal and spiritual fulfillment should best lead. Ken Blanchard observes that while civilizations have consistently created leadership structures that are pyramidal in nature with power exerted from the top, Jesus turned this pyramid upside down. He chose to place himself and those who would lead His kingdom at the bottom and the interest and needs of others above them. When asked difficult questions such as, How do I become first? or Who is the greatest? Jesus' philosophy about true leadership was pristinely clear: "If anyone wants to be first, he must be the very last, and the servant of all" (Mark 9:35).[38]

Jesus: The Ultimate Servant Leader

Stacy Rinehart maintains that Jesus turned aspiring leaders' common assumptions and values about leadership upside down through His revolutionary teachings about servant leadership. Jesus' view of leadership is what Rhinehart calls the paradox of servant leadership. More than a nice addendum to a long list of leadership ideals, Jesus' servant leadership concept defies modern concepts of power, authority, and control and releases the leader to a pattern of leadership that embraces deep humility, disregards personal interests as a motivation for leadership, and puts others first.

Jesus' teachings cut through the superfluous issues of current leadership practices and moves quickly to the heart of the matter, addressing the motives and values that drive Christian leadership practices. His teachings still serve as templates for a leadership model that will best nurture and preserve God's church in the world.

Bickering disciples prompted Jesus to share some of His most revolutionary insights about effective leadership. Just prior to the disciples' argument about who would be the greatest in their anticipated kingdom, Jesus had prophetically shared about His imminent betrayal, death, and resurrection. Incredibly, the power-hungry disciples either did not understand what He was saying or did not care that their teacher was soon to die. Some even suggest that the ensuing discussion about who would be greatest was prompted by the thought of Jesus' death and which one of them would replace Him! When asked why they were arguing, they held their peace, perhaps too embarrassed to tell the truth. Jesus then shared a teaching that would force a rethinking of the issues and values that characterize a true Christian leader.

The Enduring Principle of True Christian Leadership

Jesus, responding to His disciples' mistaken notions about leadership, assumed the sitting position of a rabbi and called His disciples to Him. "If anyone wants to be first, he must be the very last, and the servant of all" (Mark 9:35). Jesus' use of the term "servant" *(diakonos)* would clearly communicate to His disciples. The word emphasizes the attention given in the service of another and carries the idea of devotion. Frankly, the disciples were probably puzzled by this initial lecture on how to climb to the top of the leadership ladder. Their thinking embraced the conventions of the day. *If I lead, I am served by others,* they would have reasoned. Jesus quickly turned this thinking upside down. The most striking characteristic of effective leaders is devoted service to others, service that focuses thoroughly on the needs, personal growth, and happiness of others.

Core Ideals for the Servant Leader

Jesus poignantly illustrated the quintessential behaviors of the servant leader. He gave three successive teachings that form the core of servant-leadership behaviors and attitudes.

Jesus took a child in His arms and said, "Whoever welcomes one of these little children in my name welcomes me; and whoever welcomes me does not welcome me but the one who sent me" (Mark 9:37). The key word of this statement is "welcome" *(dechomai)*. The word denotes a deliberate and ready reception and favor on behalf of the subject. The leadership lesson here is not complicated: The servant leader sees all people as equals to himself or herself. Jesus illustrated this by welcoming a child who would have nothing of consequence or value to give the leader. Jesus was saying, "If you welcome those who have little or nothing to give, you welcome me and God."

The practical implications of this teaching are clear. A leader's attitude toward those who have no influence and cannot enhance a leader's status by personal association with the leader must be viewed and treated the same as those who could enhance favorable perceptions of the leader. Jesus taught that the less fortunate should be an object of special attention and ministry. Ignoring those marginalized by society is tantamount to ignoring Jesus himself. The practical admonitions of James urge a servant like attitude toward all members of the local congregation, whether rich or poor (James 2:1-11). A basic understanding of total equality in the body of Christ inspired the primitive church to continually make provisions for the less fortunate among them (Acts 2:42-45; 6:1-4).

Jesus continued to build His description of true greatness when apparently John intuitively realized the disciples had made an error by rebuking an individual who had been exorcising demons by Jesus' authority, but was not a part of their circle of fellowship. "Teacher," said John, "we saw a man driving out demons in your name and we told him to stop, because he was not one of us" (Mark 9:38). Perhaps John was wondering what they had done when they stopped this individual. After all, even little children who have no real influence or power were to be received without reservation or question.

"Do not stop him," Jesus said (Mark 9:39). Jesus then explained His response. Sincere individuals could not perform miracles in His name and in the next moment be against Him. Although an individual may stand outside an accepted circle, authenticity of the act is gauged by the person's true commitment to the cause. Such individuals will receive God's blessing and approval, even for the smallest act of kindness (vv. 19-41). The leadership lesson in this episode is critical where exclusivity is an acceptable practice: The servant leader graciously accepts the good work of others who minister outside the circle of familiar faces and methods. Moreover, the servant leader rejoices in the effectiveness of others' work and its potential reward. Jesus said others do not necessarily need to meet specified definitions of orthodoxy to be vindicated by the apparent blessing of God. True leaders see beyond the walls of convention and orthodoxy and express acceptance and appreciation for the praiseworthy ministries of others.

Jesus had one more principle to impart as He continued to hone His definition of true greatness in leadership. He began by issuing a warning against those who cause "little ones" to sin: "If anyone causes one of these little ones who believe in me to sin, it would be better for him to be thrown into the sea with a large millstone tied around his neck" (Mark 9:42). He then reintroduced a radical teaching that He had shared earlier with His disciples: "If your hand causes you to sin, cut if off...if your foot causes you to sin, cut it off...if your eye causes you to sin, pluck it out" (vv. 43-47). A body that is infirm or mutilated is preferable to a life without discipline! The servant leader must live a disciplined and obedient life and constantly think about the eternal consequences of his or her actions, particularly when the tender faith of others is at stake.

Mark's strategic collage of leadership lessons vividly illustrates how Jesus turned the world's power paradigm upside down. Effectively utilizing this brief series of events, Jesus scored direct hits on His disciples' immature thinking and inordinate ambition for position and power and at the same time illustrated acceptable attitudes and behaviors of the truly great leader. Acceptable attitudes and behaviors toward unimportant people—those considered outsiders—and Christ's most humble followers demonstrate a mature understanding of servant leadership.

Leighton Ford suggests that critical questions emerge from this trilogy of leadership lessons that serve to illustrate leadership greatness:

> Not "How many people help me?" but "How deep is my commitment to others?" Not "Whom do I let into my circle of influence?" but, "How long and broad is my circle of fellowship. Whom can I include and still be loyal to Jesus?" Not "How can I best develop myself?" but, "How intense is my passion to be pure and useful?"[39]

Servant leaders must seriously reflect on the obvious and implied leadership attitudes and behaviors that are underscored through Mark's series of events. Motives and methods must bear the weight of incisive, diagnostic questions that seek to discover the interior flaws of well-intentioned leaders.

Jesus and Issues of Power

How should the servant leader define power in terms of leadership effectiveness? How does the servant leader exercise power in leadership roles? What are the legitimate sources of power for servant leaders? These questions form the framework of Jesus' teaching about power in the lives of His disciples.

In a memorable incident, reported in two of the Gospels, Jesus spoke to issues of power in leadership. The passages clearly reveal that a servant's heart will be conveyed through a servant's method.

James and John and their mother requested that her sons be given key power positions in the coming Kingdom. The request incensed the other ten disciples, but Jesus wisely used this moment to speak of the true nature of leadership within the fellowship of the Church. Jesus compared secular leadership methods against the leadership methods of servant leaders within the Church.

> You know that the rulers of the Gentiles lord it over them, and their high officials exercise authority over them. Not so with you, whoever wants to become great among you must be your servant, and whoever wants to be first must be your slave—just as the Son of Man did not come to be served, but to serve, and to give his life as a ransom for many.[40]

This passage may be Jesus' seminal teaching about leadership within the Church. Attacking most ingrained presumptions about leadership, Jesus in effect creates a new leadership culture that will distinguish leadership in His church from the modes and attitudes of leadership in the world.

The apparent contrasts of worldly leadership with kingdom leadership greatly assist in understanding how the servant-leader model can work in cultures in which common power models are accepted. Richards and Hoeldtke suggest that the preceding passage contains at least thirty contrasts and comparisons. In *A Theology of Church Leadership,* they note the following: the worldly model puts leaders "over" those they rule, but church leadership has a relationship with the led, the servant is "among" those he or she leads. The worldly model is based upon "command" and "authority," but the servant model would find such thinking repulsive and untenable, simply because servants are not commanders. Rather than tell, the servant shows. The secular leader can call upon sanctions for response to leadership efforts, but the servant solicits desired behavior through the deeper inner forces that culminate in commitment and response. One style mandates behavioral conformity, the other style invites heart commitment. A wider range of coercive means is available to the secular authoritarian leader, but in the church of Christ the power to coerce or cajole behaviors is soundly rejected.[41] The servant leader finds his or her power base not in authority conferred by others, but in the magnetism and power of the life fully dedicated to the service of others.

What We Want Versus What We Get

The Gospel of Mark records James' and John's request for power, but with an additional and important aspect. After hearing the request for one to sit on the left and the other to sit on the right when Christ attained His glory, Jesus gave an insight regarding how the ability to lead comes into the believer's experience. Jesus' answer, according to Mark, may have startled the two disciples, "You don't know what you are asking," Jesus said. "Can you drink the cup I drink or be baptized with the baptism I am baptized with?" (Mark 10:38). It seems James and John understood the metaphors involved. The cup typified wrath and baptism God's displeasure with sin. Nearness to Jesus in glory had its price in this life. Apparently Jesus was saying, "If you share in my glory, you will first share in my suffering and death."

The two ambitious disciples understood and Jesus prophetically confirmed the history and death and exile that would follow their lives: "You will drink the cup I drink and be baptized with the baptism I am baptized with, but to sit at my right or left is not for me to grant. *These places belong to those for whom they have been prepared*" (Mark 10:39-40, emphasis mine). According to Ford, this statement infers that leadership in the Kingdom involves a sovereign assignment. He observes, "Leadership is a call from God, not a position we choose for ourselves."[42]

The servant leader understands the need for preparation, but there is a clear difference between preparation for sharing life in service and blatantly seeking promotions. According to Mark, this was the occasion that led to Jesus' fundamental teaching just cited. Mark's version can be summarized: Leadership involves God's sovereign choice in terms of whom He appoints to key positions and suffering and struggling is essential to the varied experiences that come to leaders and ultimately lead to intimacy with God. With little thought of the cultural power accruements that normally come to leaders, Christ's disciples simply serve.

A Transforming Symbolism for Servant Leaders

Poling and Miller, seeking to discover relevant and continuing foundations for a theology of ministry in a contemporary culture, believe that a credible and effective church ministry goes beyond education that prepares the church leader for specialization and professionalization. Their questions, at the very least, are evocative. What is the difference between specialized ministries and their secular counterparts outside the church? What is Christian about ministry whose guiding images come from the professions in the surrounding society? They conclude that the church's gains in professionalization may in fact lead to the loss of integrity in ministry.[43]

Poling and Miller follow their concerns to an illuminating conclusion. They contend that ministry is leadership that is "called and trained to serve the community of faith in its local activities" and its outreach to the world. They envision community formation taking place with an atmosphere where varied ministry skills are practiced and the ministry finds a willingness to do many things to bring a theological interpretation of its life to the world.[44]

The call to do many things to interpret the Christian life to the world finds deep roots in one of Jesus' final gestures toward His disciples. John recorded the stirring incident in chapter 13 of his gospel. The story that unfolds is assigned an incredibly important place in John's thought. He stated that Jesus' washing His disciples' feet is an integral aspect of the purposeful love of Christ for His earthly disciples, reflecting "the full extent of his love for them" (John 13:1-2). This servant-gesture both defined and reflected the all-encompassing love of Christ for his disciples. Simply stated, the extent of Christ's love motivated Him to fill the role of a servant as a symbolic declaration of His absolute love for His own.

During the evening meal, Jesus employed the imagery of a servant by performing the menial task of washing feet—something that no one else would do before the meal began. Girded with the towel of humility and bearing the basin of gentle service to His fellows, Jesus deliberately and humbly moved toward His disciples (John 13:1-15). This was a lesson of humility and anticipated His ultimate act of selfless love—the Cross. Jesus' servant tutorial exemplified the sacrificial love of the Passover Lamb and powerfully set forth the principle of selfless service that is to characterize those who follow His example. An act of deep humility and complete love sealed the meaning of Christian love in the hearts and minds of the disciples.

Some Christians argue that Christ intended to institute a foot-washing service ordinance to be practiced in His church. The more reasonable explanation is that Christ's humble service to His disciples has a wider and more profound significance. The deep love of all Christians, particularly Christian leaders, should make them willing to perform acts of menial service for one another.

> Now that I, your Lord and Teacher, have washed your feet, you also should wash one another's feet. I have set you an example that you should do as I have done for you. I tell you the truth, no servant is greater than his master.... Now that you know these things, you will be blessed if you do them.[45]

Leaders serve their followers, and the leader himself or herself becomes a follower of the highest law of love (James 2:8). This is the law that insists that Christian leaders stand ready on all occasions and under every circumstance to serve and bear one another's burdens and thereby flesh out the ultimate meaning of Christian love (Gal. 6:2). Christ's exemplary act of overpowering service to His fellows begs a most intriguing question for the servant leader: How may I best serve those whom I lead?

Serving Love

Jesus' understanding of leadership hinged on His full apprehension of serving love. An overpowering love for God would enable a faithful service to God's laws and bring a unique revelation of God into the disciples' lives (John 14:15-21). This unique cadre of leaders would evidence a single identifying mark that could be immediately identified by even the most disinterested outsider—serving love (13:34-35).

According to Jesus, singular acts of serving love possess the power of a compelling and convincing witness to the outsider. Jesus illustrated this transforming principle by the gift of His own life as a sacrifice for the sins of humanity. What Jesus has done on the Cross cannot and should not be repeated. There is, however, the unceasing need to continue in the serving acts of love that Jesus said would characterize His followers. A contemporary servant leader is asked to perform a thousand deeds of kindness and service toward those needful among them.

The Church As Servant

Shortly before entering Jerusalem for the last time, Jesus promised His disciples that His church would be built (Matt. 16:18). Luke would become the primitive church historian that would record the manner in which Jesus would fulfill this promise to His disciples. The Book of Acts is the recorded history of God's methodology for building the New Testament church. Although much of Acts is specific to the culture in which the Church was born and flourished, much of the corporate dynamism that served to nurture the Early Church is pertinent to the contemporary Church worldwide. Many exciting principles of church growth may be readily extracted and applied to the church world today. Although many relevant themes may be drawn from a study of the first-century Church, the servanthood of believers is one of the most significant aspects of the Early Church that mandates duplication today.

Jesus modeled the life of a servant and told His disciples that they must do the same (Mark 9:33-36; John 13:1-13). At the end of time when nations are judged, followers of Christ will be held accountable to a servant lifestyle that addresses the particular needs of the downtrodden, the poor, and the forgotten (Matt. 25:31-46). It is apparent that a general attitude of servanthood is to permeate the Church. There is nothing in Scripture to indicate that the contemporary Church can give only lip service to concepts of servanthood and servant leadership and make a passing grade.

Jesus did not spend time preparing for His twelve disciples to create and administrate an organization. He was, however, vitally interested in building a sense of community among them. He prayed that they might be one and carry out a highly unified work in a fragmented world (John 17). Jesus foresaw a close and continuing fellowship that would bring others into its divine health and warmth while at the same time effectively addressing the needs of the world through the power of the Father (Matt. 18:19-20).

Christ fortified His philosophy of servanthood through the methodology and teachings of His own life. His leadership style was that of a servant, although He possessed all power in heaven and earth. Jesus insisted that the most important part of the Torah dealt with loving and caring relationships in which servanthood could flourish, a position that threatened the religious elite of the day.[46] Jesus ultimately defined servanthood through His redemptive death (20:28). The giving of himself to others in ministry and dying became the standard by which a small group of followers would seek to discover their personal and corporate relevance to their world.

The Inception and Growth of the Servant Church

After the birth of the Church on the Day of Pentecost, early church leaders gave themselves to the task of fleshing out the vital aspects of the faith given them by Christ. Empowered and enlightened by the Spirit, their methods were divinely driven. Their energies were devoted to building up God's people and preserving the fellowship of the growing group of disciples (Acts 2:42-47; 4:32-37). Countering the culture of the day, women were given respect and carried out significant ministries under the Spirit's empowerment. The ministry of the apostles flowed from a desire to serve, not to dominate. They did not, for the most part, endeavor to create hierarchical structures that would guarantee their survival amid human attacks and theological error. Instead, they relied on the Spirit to preserve them and lead them into the truth of God's purpose and will.[47]

The primitive church leaders continued the vision of Jesus: to build an abiding community of faith that could serve each succeeding generation. "You are no longer strangers and aliens, but fellow citizens…you too are being built together to become a dwelling in which God lives by his Spirit."[48]

Against the norms of the culture, the Church became a place of equalization for its constituents. Leadership chose to emulate Jesus' example by serving the body of Christ. No meetings were given to discussing organization structure. Flowcharts were not created. There was a sense that the Spirit was in control, guiding the leadership who themselves chose the role of servant to the fledging movement.

The Dynamics of the Servant Church

The leaders of the first-century Church were instrumental in establishing precedent for a servant-leadership approach to all matters related to the development of a meaningful ecclesiology. Stacy Rhinehart observes:

> Surely Paul and the apostles strongly considered the use of tight organizational control and the use of power and authority to produce the desired results. Whatever their considerations, they chose to emulate Jesus' example of serv-

> ing and teaching. They served the saints by confronting the false doctrines and leaders with Truth. Real power lay in the nature of God, who took on human form, died, and rose again. The saints responded because the Spirit empowered them and guided them into all truth.[49]

This group of Spirit-empowered leaders reflected the deep humility and high sense of sacrificial service that had characterized their Master. Peter, for example, viewed himself as a "fellow-elder" among those he led (1 Pet. 5:1). Peter's attitude toward servanthood formed the basis of his understanding of ministry. The fabric of ministry as woven by the Holy Spirit in local church settings will, according to Peter, ultimately manifest itself in a servant motif. Peter wrote, "Each one should use whatever gift he has to serve others, faithfully administering God's grace in its various forms."[50]

Paul also understood the vital role of the servant leader in the church. In a definitive manner, he wrote of the specific ways in which leaders serve others. The five leadership categories in Eph. 4:11 have the responsibility to "equipping God's people" (Eph. 4:7-16). New Testament leadership serves those in the body of Christ through equipping them for their own lives of service. According to Cedar, the word "equipping" in the Greek text means to make whole, to restore that which is missing, or to mend that which is broken. Servant leaders are called to minister to broken, hurting, incomplete people by building, healing, and encouraging them with the grace and love of Jesus Christ.[51]

Paul's understanding of the leadership function of equipping believers flowed from his belief that leadership functioned to create servants:

> It was he who gave some to be apostles, some to be prophets, some to be evangelists, and some to be pastors and

teachers, *to prepare God's people for works of service,* [emphasis mine] so that the body of Christ might be built up.[52]

A number of New Testament words and the regular use of their vivid imagery convey the deep commitment of the first-century leaders to develop servants in the kingdom of God. The following examples illustrate how this servanthood originated in the heart of God and enjoyed benevolent expression in the life of the Church as believers interacted with one another. The English word "deacon" *(diakonos)* referred to the lowly chore of waiting on tables. The Book of Acts describes the selection of the first deacons who were to deliver food to the hungry.[53] The idea of Spirit-empowered testimony and meaningful service were wed in the person of Stephen, one of the first deacons chosen to serve the Church.

Another term, *leitourgia,* from which comes our term "liturgy," and its derivatives form a group of terms that have a great deal of significance to Christian service. In New Testament times *leitourgein* was the term for the service that a priest offered in the temple of the gods. Early Christians successfully borrowed the term to demonstrate important shades of meaning reflected in Christian service. The term was used for services rendered by one individual to another. Paul uses *leitourgein* or *leitourgia* when referring to an offering for the poor saints of Jerusalem (Rom. 15:7; 2 Cor. 9:12). The word was also applied to specific religious service (Luke 1:23; Acts 13:2). The high priestly work of Jesus was seen as a special service accomplished on behalf of humankind (Heb. 8:2, 6).

Leitourgia holds significance for the Christian servant. Paul used it of himself when he spoke of himself as Jesus Christ's *leitourgos* to the Gentiles (Rom. 15:16). In time, the term was applied to the essential work that individuals carried out for God. This nuance of meaning unfolded a powerful truth regarding Christian service. Specifically, all that the individual did for God was a "liturgy" assigned to men by God, and the most common task was glorious because it was done for Him. These shades of meaning lead Barclay to observe: "The Christian is a man who works for God and men, first because he desires to, with his whole heart, and second, because he is compelled to, because the love of Christ constrains him."[54]

The phrase translated "reasonable worship (or service)" in Rom. 12:1 is translated from *latreia.* Brown believes the term could be applied to hired servants, and acknowledges that some feel the term represents the lowliest of the low.[55] The application of the term involves the worshiper coming before God with a deep sense of humility.

The most commonly used word is that which is applied to a slave: *doulos.* This word, like all other New Testament terms related to servants, rings with the quality of humility and the decision to serve God and others through the most menial tasks. *Doulos* was a term for slave. Many translations use the word "slave" while others euphemistically translate the term "servant." The term was a favorite with Paul, and he used it to describe his service to God and the service of those who would follow his example (Rom. 1:1; 1 Cor. 7:22; 2 Cor. 4:5; Phil. 2:22). Another word related to the servant motif was one used of a person who gave public service, similar to that of a contemporary civil servant.

Servants and the Emerging Kingdom of God

Like the servants of the New Testament, those who have followed Jesus in succeeding centuries are compelled to have an adequate understanding of the kingdom of God and how it finds presence and relevance in the modern world. First, when Scripture refers to God's kingdom, it always refers to His reign, His rule, and His sovereignty. When this is understood, the New Testament comes alive with many passages where the kingdom of God is not a realm or even a people, but God's reign.[56]

How do biblical servants relate to God's reign on earth? Indeed, what role do biblical servants play in fulfilling Jesus prayer, "Thy kingdom come, thy will be done on earth is it is in heaven"? This prayer is an invitation for God to reign, to display His sovereignty and power, and to establish His rule on earth. Where do servants fit into this marvelous picture of God establishing His reign of peace and joy today?

Howard Snyder suggests that understanding the Kingdom as model can be helpful for Christians endeavoring to understand how the universal Church and the individual relate to and function within the kingdom of God. Postulating eight models for the kingdom of God, Snyder seeks to understand the basic issues of God's saving work in the world today. Among his models, the Kingdom as a counter-system offers some understanding of the servant role within God's kingdom. Offering the asset of an actual social community that literally shares life together day by day under the flag of a "new social reality," the counter-system loses much of its appeal to contemporary American culture. On the other hand, the strong emphasis upon faithful witness through servanthood strikes a true chord for those currently living under the reign of God. This perspective of the model suggests that Christians are called not to bring in the Kingdom but to serve the King in humble faithfulness with full assurance that God's kingdom will come in God's manner at God's time. Until the Kingdom fully comes, Christians most effectively serve the kingdom of God through serving those around them.[57]

It is important to understand that Jesus meant for all to be invited to enter God's kingdom. The Kingdom comes as a magnanimous gift and is entered not by good or noble deeds, but through repentance and the acceptance of God's forgiveness (Matt. 8:3; Luke 18:9-14). Later, Jesus' disciples continued His vision of bringing God's kingdom into the hearts of individuals. Beyond the message of the Kingdom, the disciples began framing God's view of the Kingdom through the window of community and service. They would continue Jesus' work by perpetuating His new community of the forgiven. Where sin and brokenness had destroyed God's loving reign on earth, the servants of God would lift the eyes of the people to a better way of life—life under the reign of Christ.

This message of the Kingdom had special relevance to the poor (Luke 6:20-21). Sider contends that one cannot understand Jesus' teaching on the Kingdom unless it is understood that the breaking through of God's kingdom on earth was particularly relevant to the poor. Consequently, proclamation must include elements of the messianic spirit that endeavors to serve the marginalized, weak, and socially ostracized of the world.[58]

If the kingdom is now and strongly relates to the broken and downtrodden, the practical implications of Christian servanthood are many. Sider contends,

> One simply does not understand Jesus' teaching on the Kingdom unless one sees that He was especially concerned that the poor realize that the Kingdom breaking into history was particularly good news for them. Our proclamation of the gospel is simply unbiblical unless we, like Jesus, focus special attention on the poor.[59]

Snyder, visualizing the Church as community, and therefore a sign of the kingdom of God, encourages the Church to walk in those good works that were characteristic of Christ's work on earth. He too gives the charismatic Church a compelling mandate to evangelize the world, with special attention to the poor and oppressed. Specific human need is met and those who have no social power find a voice and acceptance when the Church serves its Lord through acts of love and kindness on behalf of the poor.

Although serving the poor and meeting specific human need is not the primary or exclusive task of the Church, serving acts is a testimony that the redemption and holiness of the Church include every area of life.[60]

At the heart of the Church as kingdom is the issue of mission. In fact, the nature of God's advancing Kingdom demands that the Church gives itself to kingdom tasks—those critical matters drawn to the Church's attention by the Spirit's work within it.[61] Missiological renewal—an awareness of God's redemptive plan in the world and the Church's place in it—is a vital aspect of church renewal. Such a renewal of mission and vision may begin when a church engenders a new ministry in the local church, the neighborhood, or the world.[62]

A Theology of Relationship: A Foundation For Servant Leadership

The biblical theme of relationship offers a fresh view of God's design for spiritual leadership that assumes the role of a caring servant. The mystical meld of the Trinity offers a compelling example of both unity and diversity in relationship that ultimately contributes to function and purpose. The relationship of the personalities of the Trinity demonstrates fundamental principles regarding leadership. These striking principles and characteristics of the unified Godhead are articulated by Rhinehart:

> What we see in the Godhead is an incredible picture of interdependence, and of unity and diversity, where the One leading and the One being led change according to need and contribution. Equality is the basis of their relationship, yet there is also role differentiation among the Trinity. They share authority, yet each has a special function. There is no jealousy of competition in their midst—only harmony and unity.[63]

These realities of the Trinity's union, operation, and interrelationship have relevance to the servant leader. Unity and diversity are not mutually exclusive among leaders. Leadership has its roots in relationships, not organization or hierarchy. Those things that destroy relationships—jealously, ambition, competition, and power struggles—must be eliminated. Shared authority is a concept that needs conscious development in churches. Leaders listen to and learn from one another. It is imperative that leaders squelch any sense of superiority among themselves.[64]

An overarching theme of Scripture, particularly the New Testament, is the relationship of leaders to those they lead. Richards and Hoeldtke contend that the responsibility of church leaders in not to manage the church, but to give care and nurture to believers. Human leaders express their gifts and callings to move the congregation toward spiritual maturity and meaningful relationships in which Jesus can speak and individuals respond. This is the heart of Eph. 4:12, which casts the leader in the role of equipping *(katartismos),* literally translated, "to straighten out the disjointed." Putting the body in order for ministry, growth, and service to God and the world is the driving force behind the gifts and callings of leadership.[65]

Relationships in the body of Christ must also be understood in vertical terms, that is, the relationship of the believer to God. As the church offers service to its members, the Holy Spirit manifests himself through members of the body of Christ and there is a transforming release of God's power within believers (2 Cor. 3:18). This release of God's power expresses itself in a special giftedness that flows among members of a local body of believers (1 Cor. 12-14) and culminates in practical expressions of love (1 Cor. 13) and other enabling activities characterized by a mutual sharing of burdens (12:25-26).

First Among Equals: A New Testament Pattern for Servant Leadership

How can the Church best utilize its human and material resources within a culture? Greenleaf envisions the role of the church going far beyond its four walls. Based upon his conclusion that churches no longer act as strong reference points for value formation in culture, he poses a question that anticipates the church coming into a significant role in providing servant leadership that will eventually permeate other institutions: If some of the churches do not accept the opportunity to build leadership strength for other institutions that have greater value-shaping influence on individuals than the church now has, how will the churches do their work?[66]

Greenleaf cites two events in history that he believes have betrayed the servant leadership model for church leadership. He contends that although Martin Luther's break with the Catholic church affirmed the priesthood of the believer, the Reformation did not devise a role for the pastor that would permit the development of the laity into functioning priests or servants. A century later, the well-intentioned George Fox founded the Quakers. Greenleaf contends Fox's efforts fell short because this group dispensed with the pastor altogether, leaving the church as a pastorless flock that could not grow or adapt to its surroundings.[67] Therefore, a fundamental response for a growing-edge church is to learn what neither Luther nor Fox knew: the need to build a church of equals in which strong leadership with an empowered, serving board and a pastor who functions as *primus inter pares*—first among equals.[68] Such an arrangement, according to Greenleaf, would empower the church to influence individuals in its ranks, who in turn would lift the values of the culture around them. Furthermore, Greenleaf believes that a church that encourages servant leadership among equals could become the central conceptual resource that would serve as a model for a more just, a more loving, and a more serving society.

Even though many churches may not accept all the methods and conclusions espoused by Greenleaf, it does seem apparent that the primitive Church operated on a strong basis of servant leadership, and key leaders viewed church leadership in a manner significantly different from many contemporary pastors and church leaders. The very nature of servant leadership insists that a contemporary church leader reflect in attitudes and leadership behaviors the heart of a true servant.

If the training manual for servant leadership within the church is Scripture, then a wealth of instruction awaits the aspiring servant leader. Two key words used for the leadership in the New Testament were *presbuteros* and *episkopos*. *Presbuteros* is commonly translated "elder," literally, an older person respected by the public because of the wisdom and maturity that comes with age. Generally translated "bishop," *episkopos* is indicative of one who takes oversight of a church and serves as a key pastor. Another term *poimen* is translated "pastor" (Latin) or "shepherd," reflecting a commonly used New Testament image of the church leader. Other general understandings of first-century leadership are terms such as "leader" (Rom. 12:8), and "administrator" (I Cor. 12:28). Scripture also employs general phraseology to capture the work of leaders: "those...over you in the Lord" (I Thess. 5:12) and "those who have rule over you" (Heb. 13:7).[69]

It appears that the free and interchangeable use of general terms precluded the idea of looking at leadership in a technical sense in the first-century Church. This seems to agree with Griffiths who says of early biblical leadership, "The only general conclusion is that, while there is always officially recognized authority and leadership that is to be respected and obeyed, the actual title used and the mode of organization are quite different."[70]

What is apparent in the Early Church was the lack of leadership based in organizational power or authority with the ability to act coercively or in a cajoling manner.

An examination of two New Testament passages seems to confirm Griffiths conclusion. First Peter 5:1-2 indicates that the elder, pastor, and bishop were various aspects of one office. This seems also true in Paul's final statement to the pastoral elders of the Ephesians' church in Acts 20:25-35. Essentially, New Testament pastoral leadership worked from a servant base, combining the concepts of elder, bishop, and pastor into a single profile of a strong, decisive, but gentle leader who shepherded the flock of God, a kind of *primus inter pares*—first among equals.

A strong servant disposition is a critical element in serving the body of Christ. The temptation to love the crowd, more than loving the people in it, is a danger. There may be more glamour in working as executive, leader, or preacher, but the litmus test of servant leadership is entering into relationships that cast the pastor in the role of friend, confidant, and adviser.

Mission

The Church in North America is the product of two millennium of organizational tradition. Tradition often serves the Church well, while at other times it can become an impediment to missionary growth and vision. The challenge lies partially in the ability of contemporary church leadership to preserve time-honored and proven traditions that are valuable to the church, while at the same time allowing the Holy Spirit and Scripture to guide in the formation of a missional community that serves both the world at large and those in the redeemed community. The search by leadership to create a truly missional community begins with God's biblical intent for the Church and then strategizing to empower the Church to carry out that intent. Strategies that bring the Church into meaningful missional engagement with culture will be contoured by the exceptional diversity of biblical images for that church which creatively informs the church at any time in history.[71]

The biblical image of a servant church can empower the contemporary church in a time when many traditional and biblical values are in question. The servant church is a natural expression of God's great grace toward individuals and the work of His grace within individuals. An essential aspect of the work of grace within the church is the unity that should come naturally to the company of Christian servants. Scripture admonishes Christians to live life "in a manner worthy of the gospel of Christ" (Phil. 1:27). The highly unified nature of a servant community can be illustrated by a recurrent Pauline term, *allelon* (one another, each other).[72] According to Paul, Christianity is a powerful corporate affair in which the servant attitude manifests itself through a body of servants who share a mutual care for one another.

Christian faith is not an individual matter; everything is to be done with and for one another. Within the community of those who live "in Christ" by the power of the Holy Spirit, persons are to be "members one of another" (Rom. 12:5, KJV), "build up each other" (1 Thess. 5:11), "love one another with mutual affection" (Rom. 12:10, KJV), "able to instruct one another" (15:14, KJV), "live in harmony with one another" (12:16), and "become slaves to one another" (Gal. 5:13, KJV).[73]

The Church is under a mandate to express the fullness of God's redemptive love within the context of the servant community as well as the larger culture in which community exists. The corporate life of the Church must embody a noble social order that is clearly indicative of God's redemptive purposes in the world. When a practical ministry of service flows from the center of the church's life to the culture around it, the servant church becomes light and salt to the world.

The Balance and Effectiveness of the Biblical Models of Leadership

From a scriptural perspective, the concept of leader as servant is not a solitary or isolated view of leadership. Although it may be said that Scripture upholds and promotes the servant leader perspective as foundational to all leadership thinking, other images or models of leadership and ministry are furnished to demonstrate the balanced view that is essential to effective leadership. This reality helps dispel some of the criticism that a servant leader is too "soft" for the workplace. A consideration of the following three biblical models provides the contemporary Christian leader with the essential understanding that leadership comprises a variety of circumstances and challenges that require versatility and creativity in the modern world.

The Servant Model

The servant concepts are fundamental to the understanding of the underlying spiritual life of the leader. Perhaps more than any other aspect of leadership, the servant role may best affirm the level of spiritual intimacy that the servant enjoys with the Master. In this respect, the servant role becomes the fountainhead from which all other aspects of meaningful ministry flow. Fundamental life attitudes and the ministerial habits and behaviors that grow from them are the true reflections of the level of servanthood within the individual.

The private spiritual life and the public ministry life of the Christian leader gravitates around the single but powerful idea of servant leader. The concept of servant leader and the attitudes and characteristics it entails are clearly if passionately conveyed in Scripture. Four Greek words form a rather comprehensive understanding of the calling and tasks of the servant leader.

A *diakonos* is a worker and stands in relation to what the servant is asked to do. *Diakonos* represents the work that the servant is required to do. Generally speaking, this category of servant was applied to the free servant usually working in a domestic situation as a guard, attendant, or messenger. There is often a sense of deep devotion and affection associated with the term. The *diakonos* leader is one who clearly understands the responsibilities that have been given and affectionately carries them out for the welfare of Christ and His kingdom. Tasks are readily accepted and a sense of joy attends the manner and work of the *diakonos* leader.[74]

A *doulos* is a slave and emphasizes the servant's accountability to his master.[75] The *doulos* leader recognizes the ownership of the master and does not seek in any way to free himself or herself from it. In fact, it is a relationship of deep commitment in which the slave would not choose freedom even if it were possible. This relationship is marked by the great love and commitment of the servant to the master. There is no wish to be free or go one's own way. The guiding passion is the unconditional dedication of the one serving.

A *huperetes* is the servant in relation to his or her superior, acting and fulfilling tasks under the authority of the superior. The term literally means an "under-rower," as distinguished from *nautes*, or a seaman. The term denotes any subordinate acting under another's authority.[76] The *huperetes* leader yields to the voice of ultimate authority. This servant does not question the direction or the orders given. A keen sense of responsibility and a passion to duty characterizes the attitude of this special servant leader.

The foregoing terms catch the variegated beauty of the servant leader like the carefully cut surface of an exquisite diamond. Although the diamond is a single entity, each surface catches and refracts its own light in a unique way, adding to the beauty of the whole. The servant leader is a multidimensional leader who serves Christ and His church with an attitude of service and who continually seeks avenues of loving expression. The servant attitude is manifested in loving devotion *(diakonos)*, unconditional service *(doulos)*, and passionate accountability *(huperetes)*.

The Steward Model

If the image of servant catches the finer points of the leader's spiritual life, the image of steward frames the responsibilities of the leader's function within the church. The root of the word "steward" *(oikonomos)* is the same as the root for "manager of a household." Jesus spoke of the steward as one who manages under the direction of another, particularly the owner. The steward did not own that which he managed, but his reputation hinged on his ability to manage with integrity and prudence (Luke 16:1-8).[77]

Although Shawchuck sees stewardship and servanthood as synonymous concepts characterized in partnering relationships with organizations, he feels it is more appropriate for churches to view the concepts of servanthood and stewardship as separate dimensions of the single call to leadership. Servanthood reflects the spiritual side of the leadership enterprise, while stewardship encapsulates the functional side of leadership as duties are carried out within the organization. Stewardship embraces the values of responsibility to an organization and a vital concern for those who are a part of it. It includes a sense of ownership and responsibility for outcomes at all levels within the organization.

The concept of leader as steward is the empowering dimension of the leadership effort. Because stewards are given responsibility and held accountable, there is also a mantle of authority without which the most difficult tasks of ministry could not be completed (1 Cor. 4:1-5). The responsibility of the steward naturally includes those elements of leadership empowerment that can eventually accommodate the goals and vision of the master of the house and ensure the efficient operation of his enterprises.

The Shepherd Model

Leadership in the Church finds one of its strongest images in that of shepherd. The leader as servant manages personal spirituality and serves others as a high expression of maturing faith. The leader as steward purposefully manages God's program of ministry on this earth, recognizing heaven's resources as always being available for the task. The leader as shepherd turns his or her attention to the nurturing and protecting of the flock that God has placed under his or her care. The illustration of the pastor and the sheep, taken from the agrarian world of the Israelites, is very powerful. The role of "pastor" (Latin for *shepherd*) in the life of the sheep is awesome. It is the responsibility of a nurturing pastor to feed the flock of God and protect them from harmful outside influences (Acts 20:28-31). Jesus set the ultimate standard of a loving shepherd, showing himself as the example of love and sacrifice that is necessary for caring pastoral ministry (John 10:1-18). The apostle Paul viewed the call of pastor-teacher as essential to the spiritual and intellectual maturation of the Church (Eph. 4:9-16).

The modern pastor approaches ministry with an understanding that leading is both functioning as a steward and ministering as a servant. In the role of pastor, the leader finds those who can assist and bring a full complement of ministries into the body of Christ. The pastor fills a multiplicity of roles and, when needed, calls other shepherds to his or her side to fulfill the responsibilities of teaching, praying, serving, ruling, correcting, and other duties that characterize the New Testament role of pastor.[78]

Patterns of servant leadership in the Early Church were more matters of practical function than titles of power or authority. The terms applied to leadership function were simple extensions of the culture in which the Church was born and matured. Some of the terms had been used for leaders in Judaism (e.g., "elder"), and others were borrowed from Greek culture.[79] A term was applied because it described an emerging leadership function. An understanding of these elemental terms is helpful when one realizes that the infant Church was raised and matured by the power of the Holy Spirit, a process that assured the inclusion of the servant mentality and functionality among early church leaders.[80]

Servant Leaders and the Contemporary Church

Regarding critical matters of leadership in the kingdom of God, the spirit of the Gospels is clear. Jesus admonished the disciples not to strive for greatness based on position, title, or rank.[81] Instead, Jesus indicated that true greatness stems from one's ability to perceive the worth and relevance of members of society generally considered to be least important.[82] Furthermore, Jesus' notions of deep humility and dedicated service poignantly remind us that the values of His kingdom often run contrary to values found in contemporary churches.[83] A clear mandate for the contemporary Christian leader is the rediscovery of kingdom values that respect and respond to those served by leaders; practical implementation of these values in the personal life and ministry of the leader; and a thorough engraining of servant principles, attitudes, and actions within individual congregations.[84]

Servanthood and Life Context

The fundamental attitude of current servant leaders is discovered in the biblical mind-set of the hardworking and undeserving servant. Western culture and its prevailing emphasis upon the prerogatives and rights of the individual can dim within the conscience of the leader the soft light of servanthood. Biblical servants simply see themselves as those called to conduct a meaningful work within the context of their lives and ministry.[85]

Servant leaders themselves have an understanding that their life and calling are their work, a means of expressing the holiness of God within their lives. As leaders, they endeavor to lead those under their care into a similar understanding that life, calling, and vocation are all a means of reflecting the attitudes and actions of the true biblical servant. The ideals of the biblical servant invade life at every level and permeate every vocation in which the Christian servant labors. Fenhagen observes:

> The vocation of Jesus was to live in the world as humanity's Servant. This understanding is fundamental to Christian ministry. The servant image in the New Testament is not an image of weakness or subservience. It is an image that reflects the meaning of power put to its rightful use—be it on a personal level, a corporate level, or even an international level.[86]

As a matter of Christian growth and maturity, servanthood as both taught in principle and exemplified in the life of the leader, emerges as fruit of God's work of grace within the life of the believer—a discovery that the joy and relevance of life lies in our ability to share love, mercy, and justice with others in the community of the kingdom of God as well as the world around us.

The Church and Service

Brox suggests that the service ministries of the church *(diakonia)* formed as much a part of the consciousness of the Early Church as the preaching of the gospel. More appropriately, it would be better to say that service to others was regarded as one of the ways of proclaiming the truth of Jesus of Nazareth. Servanthood for others was a way of preaching a sermon without words—or instead of words.[87]

For twenty-first century leaders and their churches, *diakonia* must be a reality in which the redemption they preach expresses itself through the redemptive qualities they express. The church is called to be a kingdom community actively helping, healing, and promoting changes in the spiritual lives of individuals and in some instances encouraging and promoting changes in the secular culture around them. Like the church of the first century, modern believers should seek to give Christianity a credible and meaningful expression through concrete forms of ministry. This would naturally include ministries and actions of love toward the poor, the socially oppressed, those marginalized by prevailing cultures and attitudes, the stranger, and others who are largely forgotten or ignored.[88]

A Model to Follow

The servant life of Jesus is a life-long study for those in Christian leadership. As the Servant of Jehovah, He was anointed to bring God's liberating Kingdom into the lives of individuals (Isa.62:1-11). Christ has bequeathed to the church—His heir apparent in the world—the anointing and empowering of the Holy Spirit for the purpose of sharing the good news of the Kingdom with the rest of the world (Acts 1:8). This witness goes beyond proclamation and includes the principles of servanthood by which the Church focuses the love of God upon the agony of a world without God.[89]

The Church and the Emerging Kingdom of God

An overriding message of Scripture centers upon the Church as the means of God bringing the kingdom of God (the reign of

God) into the lives of individuals. Ushering in the kingdom of God, Jesus Christ was the decisive inbreaking of the Kingdom into human history. Jesus' delivery of the kingdom of God into human experience brought the reign of God, though not yet fully, through healings, deliverance, and personal salvation. In time, the Kingdom will fully come. At this point in redemptive history, God's kingdom is vested in individual experience and His rule established in individual hearts.

The promise of the coming Kingdom is secured in the death and resurrection of our Lord and, consequently, a promise of eternal resurrection that will bring believers into a full and final fellowship with God. Even the patterns of personal Christianity illustrate the centrality of death and resurrection as a means of bringing God's fullness and power upon humanity (Rom. 6). In the meantime, the servants of God bring the initial light of the Kingdom through the propagation of God's truth on earth. The propagation of this truth has both theological realities and practical applications within the context of Christ's church. This understanding of the Kingdom insists that the contemporary Church establish the Kingdom in practical realism and not merely promote theological idealism. The kingdom now message encourages the Church to envision servant ministries under the loving guidance of the Holy Spirit and allow God to rule on earth through carefully planned strategies of servanthood.[90]

Chapter 3
VOICES FOR SERVANT-LEADERSHIP

Definitions and Concepts of Leadership

Stogdill rightly observes that leadership is a rather sophisticated concept. Most cultures in the past expressed the idea of leadership through terms such as "king" or "chief," but the Anglo-Saxon heritage finds itself preoccupied with leadership concepts. The word "leader" appeared in the English language as early as a.d.1300, according to the Oxford English Dictionary. The term "leadership" appeared in the English language about a.d. 1800. The perennial interest in the subject of leadership has led to as many definitions about leadership as there are persons who have attempted to define the concept.[91]

Burns defines leadership as "leaders inducing followers to act for certain goals that represent the values and the motivations—the wants and the needs, the expectations and aspirations—of both leaders and followers." Burns contends that the genius of leadership therefore lies in the manner in which leaders recognize and respond to their own and their followers' needs and values.[92] Cohen, who has a particular affinity to a combat model of leadership, defines leadership as, "the art of influencing others to their maximum performance to accomplish any task, objective, or project".[93] According to Maxwell, leadership can be distilled to a single but forceful concept: influence.[94]

When the dust of leadership definitions has settled, a compelling reality remains. The classic understanding of leadership implies that the leader is still at the head of the pack and knows what needs to be done, and that people are a means to that end—the end the leader has in sight. This classic perception of leadership—described as a power over style—remains the most accepted model of leadership throughout the world.[95]

Qualities of Leaders

Many contemporary writers and researchers are endeavoring to develop models of leadership that are grounded more in a genuine concern for those led and the finer points of the human spirit. While plans, logistics, corporate earnings, and numerous other organizational realities still drive hierarchical models of leadership, many understand that classic models that represent hierarchical arrangements are inadequate for many contemporary situations. Bennis points to the virtuous side of the leader and identifies several qualities in contemporary leaders:

Guiding vision. The leader has a clear idea of what to do, personally and professionally.

Passion. A passion for life, a vocation, a profession, a course of action.

Integrity. Self-knowledge and the will to act upon what is known.

Trust. Which grows over time as a product of character and integrity.

Curiosity and daring. The leader wonders about everything and is hungry to learn, to take risks, and to try new things.[96]

The earlier studies of leadership that emphasized qualities and traits of great leaders did not seem to solve the many issues related to the understanding and practicing of good leadership. Later research focused on the situation and environment of the leader and how the leader could change things in the environment. Two important factors emerged from these studies. First, leaders initiate ideas and plans—they take the lead. Second, leaders inspire people to follow them by showing consideration. It appears that theorists have come full circle and researchers are again focusing on the qualities of the leader, particularly those qualities that make a leader effective in a given situation. An oversimplification of this approach can be narrowed to three concerns: (1) the position the leader holds, (2) the person the leader is, and (3) the process the leader employs.[97]

Another significant transition in leadership studies involves the current emphasis on transformational leadership as opposed to the theories of exchange process or transactional relationships in the workplace. Some theorists advocate that leadership as a transaction (you give me what I want and I will give you something in exchange) yield to the higher order of motivation and appeal. Transformational leadership provides a level of motivation that raises the consciousness of people concerning what they want. Transformational leaders throw away old models and look at the leadership challenge in a fresh manner. Transformational leaders change the situation, change the focus and dialogue in the environment, change rules and values when needed, talk about goals, and symbolize rather than bargain.[98]

Emerging Concepts of Servant Leadership

Entering the new millennium, the workplace is beginning to see that traditional autocratic and hierarchical modes of leadership may be yielding to a new model—one that prioritizes the personal growth and happiness of workers, improves the caring dimension of the institution, supports significant feelings of teamwork and community within the institution, and encourages personal involvement in decision making. This emerging approach to leadership and service is called servant leadership.

Admittedly, cultural understandings of servant and leader are usually thought of as opposites. The merging of the prevailing understandings of servant and leader in a creative manner does create a paradox. The paradoxical idea of the servant and leader unifying into a single and influential concept of leadership is currently sprouting in many institutions, as well as many individuals who serve in a variety of institutions. Servant leadership seems to offer hope for those wanting to enter a new era in human development and significant improvements in the way people are treated who do the work within the institution.[99]

DePree moves toward a fundamental understanding of servant leadership when he says that leadership is a concept of owing certain things to the institution. It is a way of thinking about being an institutional heir, a way of thinking about stewardship and of contrasting it with ownership. Borrowing from Robert Greenleaf, Depree also states that the art of leadership requires us to think about the leader as a steward framed in the context of important relationships: of assets and legacy, of momentum and effectiveness, of civility and values.[100] The noble idea of servant leadership is distinctly people centered and seeks to manage individuals through an applied understanding of partnership. The belief system that empowers partnership is sometimes called stewardship by some and servanthood by others.[101] Block observes that stewardship is a set of principles and practices that leads the institution into changes that brings an escalated sense of ownership and responsibility for outcomes that impact individuals on all levels of the organization.[102]

Servant leadership seems desirable in the workplace from a purely sociological perspective. Lee and Zemke contend that the baby boomer, those born between 1946 – 1964, has brought a new value to the workplace. CEO worship is out with this group and it must give way to leaders, facilitators, and sponsors. The boomer manager aspires to be first among teammates and rejects old autocratic and paternalistic models.[103] Tatum postulates that individuals in the workplace are increasingly looking for true leadership models that are significantly different from those of the past—serving models that embrace a vision of leading through serving.[104]

Servant Leadership within Various Cultures

Hofstede's examination of behaviors that govern cultures and groups could have significance in terms of what cultures may more easily assimilate the major concepts of servant leadership. Hofstede's understanding of "power distance" is an example of how some cultures would find it easier or more difficult to bring a high sense of equality within leadership and those led. Power distance, the extent to which the less powerful members of institutions within a country or culture expect and accept that power is distributed unequally, has obvious impact upon a culture's ability to accept the servant efforts of a leader or a leader's willingness to offer such gestures. When a large power distance between the leader and those led exists within a culture, there is an apparent difficulty in establishing any sense of equality within a culture that most strongly identifies with inequality between leadership and subordinates.[105]

Robert Greenleaf and Servant Leadership

Current trends that advocate servant leadership attitudes and methods have largely emerged from the influence and writings of Robert K. Greenleaf. Greenleaf was influenced by an altruistic father and the moral underpinnings of a Quaker faith. In

1970, at the age of sixty-six, he began a new career after retiring from AT&T. His last years at AT&T as vice president for management research served to sharpen his interest in the satisfaction and happiness that work brings to people's lives. His interest catapulted him into a new career that involved writing, consulting, and lecturing throughout the world. A driving force behind his lecturing and writing was his desire to build a better, more caring society.[106]

Who is the servant leader? Greenleaf veered away from an outright definition of the servant leader, but he wrote extensively about those things that characterize servant leadership in the workplace and the world:

> The servant leader is a *servant first*...it begins with the natural feeling that one wants to serve, to serve first. Then conscious choice brings one to aspire to lead. That person is sharply different from one who is leader first, perhaps because of the need to assuage an unusual power drive or to acquire material possessions. For such it will be a later choice to serve—after leadership is established. The leader-first and the servant-first are two extreme types. Between them there are shadings and blends that are part of the infinite variety of human nature.[107]

As one might imagine, Greenleaf's thought often broke away from conventional ideas about leadership and management. He envisioned the leader who operated with both conceptual and operating talents. Conceptualizing related more to the art of leading, while operating is essential to administration. Able leaders have qualities in both areas, according to Greenleaf.[108] Greenleaf forged a link between maturity and becoming. He believed that education, in particular a liberal education, can become a powerful maturing force with a depth of meaning emerging only out of the educational experience.[109]

Greenleaf had a foreboding for the youth who would one day hold the reins of leadership. As he observed the radical responses of many youth toward authority during the seventies, so many of whom "having made their awesome decision for autonomy and independence from tradition, and having taken their firm stand against injustice and hypocrisy, find it hard to convert themselves into affirmative builders of a better society."[110] Giving students a hope for the future by encouraging them to constructively pursue new leadership paradigms was essential to Greenleaf's thought. He desired a future when "leaders will bend their efforts to serve with skill, understanding, and spirit, and that followers will be responsive only to able servants who would lead them."[111] Greenleaf continues:

> A new moral principle is emerging which holds that the only authority deserving one's allegiance is that which is freely and knowingly granted by the led to the leader in response to, and in proportion to, the clearly evident stature of the leader. Those who choose to follow this principle will not casually accept the authority of existing institutions. Rather they will freely respond only to individuals who are chosen as leaders because they are proven and trusted servants. To the extent that this principle prevails in the future, the only truly viable institutions will be those that are predominately servant-led.[112]

Readers of Robert Greenleaf quickly discover that although he developed the driving ideals that serve as philosophical foundations for servant leadership thought, he did little to provide a transforming means of systematically reaching them. Page suggests it was Greenleaf's notion of a servant leader more than his model that later inspired others to develop it.[113] Current servant leadership advocates benefit from The Robert K. Greenleaf Center for Servant Leadership in Indianapolis, Indiana, which has done much to systematically develop the servant leadership model. The mission of The Robert K. Greenleaf Center "is to fundamentally improve the caring and quality of all institutions through a new approach to leadership, structure, and decision making. Servant leadership emphasizes increased service to others; a holistic approach to work; promoting a sense of community; and the sharing of power in decision making."[114]

Greenleaf's Legacy: Current Thought on Servant Leadership

Greenleaf's voice seems to get stronger with time. Popular leadership writers such as James Kouzes, Barry Posner, Shiela Murray Bethel, M. Scott Peck, Peter Senge, and Max Depree have brought a great deal of credibility to the servant leader model and its use in contemporary management environments. Lee and Zemke write: "Servant leadership emphasizes service to others, a holistic approach to work, personal development, and shared decision making—characteristics that place it squarely in the mainstream of conventional talk about empowerment, total quality and participative management."[115]

Servant leadership delves into the sensitive issues of power, position, and prestige, perhaps more than any other leadership concept. Greenleaf contends, "Servanthood is ultimately tested whenever one is with one's power."[116] The primary moral test for the leader is what he or she does with power. True servant leaders utilize power and enhance the lives of those they lead. A salient feature of Greenleaf's thought insists that leaders and institutions must raise all the people within the organization to a higher level of quality as persons and workers than they could have achieved on their own.[117] Hall maintains that an orientation to serve others does not fully comprehend the essence of servant leadership: "Doing menial chores does not necessarily indicate a servant leader. Instead a servant leader is one who invests himself or herself in enabling others, in helping them be and do their best."[118]

Theorists have longed recognized the need for interaction between management and subordinates in the workplace. Research has demonstrated that high-production leaders are proportionately effective to the time and effort given to providing reliable information for their teammates, forums for offering ideas and suggestions, training for more responsibility, and in general, showing consideration for the follower and his or her needs.[119] The proposition that the acceptable leader will provide growth opportunities for those in his or her care is fundamental to servant-leader philosophy and is a cornerstone of purposeful leadership within Christian organizations, particularly the church.[120]

Bethel, focusing on the service ethic for the benefit of others, contends that if leadership serves only the leader, failure can be expected. She writes, "Ego satisfaction, financial gain, and status can all be valuable for leaders, but if they become the only motivations, they will eventually destroy the leaders. Only when service for a common good is the primary purpose are you truly leading."[121]

Servant Leadership and the Church

Rainer has demonstrated that the high-relational models being espoused by successful corporations are also working in the church. The pastoral leadership style that combines high-task and high-relationship orientation—emphasizing relationships and getting the job done—was a dominant style among pastors of growing churches.[122] Greenleaf maintained that the growing-edge church would be characterized by seekers who understand the necessity of truly serving others, reaching beyond selfish ambition and embracing the servant life. It is the responsibility of the church to nurture such seekers and lead them to servanthood. He prophesied that these would be the builders of the future.[123]

American church culture is entering into a fresh understanding of the need to develop a responsive community of faith based largely upon the servant model. Guder asserts that the growing sense of community and a deep desire to serve demonstrated in contemporary missional churches grows from an understanding of Christian connectedness and togetherness. This is not merely an in-house blessing, but overflows to the world community as well.[124] Getz believes the motivating agent that brings the body of Christ together in various forms of serving ministry is love.[125] Poling and Miller charge pastoral leadership with the responsibility of moving the church toward community through encouraging individuals to be responsive to others within the community of faith and those outside the church. The pastor is the key to the renewal and enrichment of the serving community.[126] Unhurried and deliberate pastoral leadership takes time to facilitate a priestly service to both God's and His people.[127]

Before holistic approaches toward life and church were in vogue, Lovelace anticipated a serving church that could leaven a society with an influence that could dramatically effect social change and make the message of the gospel more believable. He envisioned government and business feeling the impact of caring, socially oriented Christians who become "social dynamite" when they act prudently toward pressing human need.[128] The strategies of the new millennium must include the dedicated work of Christ's servants who understand the poverty, disease, and death that wreak havoc on the millions of poor and neglected individuals. Those with skills who can help and will heed God's call must respond to crushing human need.[129]

The attitude of servanthood characterizes those who carry out ministry as exemplified in the life of Jesus. Jesus modeled those things that still characterize servants today: sacrificial living, the willingness to simplify life, and a personal self- emptying.[130] In the four servant songs of Isaiah, the prophet anticipates God's Servant, the Messiah, ideally fulfilling the suffering servant role to the nations.[131] Jesus demonstrated His vision for the reign of God on earth through healings, exorcisms, control over the seas, feeding hungry people, and many other compassionate miracles. Although the complete reign of God remains distant, the Church shares this horizon of hope through an impulse to minister as servants of God to a wide range of human need.[132] Nouwen understands that those who possess effective ministries of healing must also move in the same dimension, "the same broken human condition," of those needing healing.[133] Bruce's classic work on discipleship challenges the aspiring pastor to think about pastoral ministry in terms already dictated by the serving life of our Lord. Leadership in the Kingdom involves both feeding the flock and following the Great Shepherd as mere servants of Christ.[134]

Characteristics of Servant Leadership

Servant leadership follows the well-worn path that leads to a high view of individuals in the workplace. As early as the fifties, theorists like Douglas McGregor proposed the well-known Y theory view of employees, in which they encouraged leadership to view employees as responsible, ambitious, energetic, ingenious, and creative. Conversely, X theory dismissed workers as lazy, untrustworthy, and resistant to change.[135]

Over time, the positive move toward the elevated view of the individual in the workplace continued. Social scientists such as Kurt Lewin, Rensis Likert, Tom Peters, Robert Waterman, and many others maintained the high view of the employee. Individuals like Robert Greenleaf and Michael L. Ray saw the new paradigm centered in the individual and meaningful changes in the workplace proceeding from the conscious or spirit. This decidedly spiritual or inward view of individuals in the workplace has been championed by Greenleaf and others. Bausch finds this spirituality expressed in the essential idea of the inherent value of work and the creativity of the individual in the workplace. People contribute to the vision and mission of the organization only insofar that individual creativity and potential are released.[136]

Sims, venturing a definition for "servant leadership" that finds its core in the value of the individual, suggests that the servant leader is the one who "honors the personal dignity and worth of all who are led and to evoke as much as possible their own innate creative power for leadership."[137] To him, "leader" is a term describing a person's role; "servant" is a term for a person's identity.[138] Gardner observes, "In the conventional model, people want to know whether the followers believe in the leader. I want to know whether the leader believes in the followers."[139] Consequently, Gardner promotes enabling and empowering people. He believes this can be accomplished by

1. the sharing of information and opportunities for learning.
2. the sharing of power by devolving initiative and responsibility.
3. the building of confidence of followers so that they can achieve their own goals through personal effort.
4. removing barriers to the release of individual energy and talent.[140]

Fraker, reflecting on Greenleaf's criterion for a successful organization, observes that the facilitating and nurturing attitude of the CEO toward the workforce is essential to success. "People are first" is the heart for transforming leadership into a people-centered activity that is based upon Greenleaf's strong notion of *primus inter pares,* first among equals.[141] CEOs express this accommodating philosophy by internalizing new attitudes toward people and using the appropriate servant-oriented language in the corporate setting.[142] Hedges maintains that the human longing for recognition and dignity is an opportunity for a leader to leave a measurable mark in the lives of others while at the same time experiencing deep personal satisfaction.[143] Cohen's research seems to confirm the belief that a secret to motivating people is giving them the respect and recognition they feel they deserve.[144]

Leaders and institutions that value their people and wish to lead them into more productive and fulfilling lives will take time to understand human behavior and motivation to find the fit between the needs and goals of the organization and those of individual employees.[145] Kouzes and Posner believe a combination of believing in others and setting forth high expectations in the work environment creates encouragement and motivation that profits both the individuals and organization they serve.[146] Leadership dedicated to helping others discover their unique giftings creates a much higher level of motivation than mere dutiful response. More accurately, people get involved in ministry and social projects because they believe they can make a positive difference by utilizing those talents, giftings, and abilities that leaders have helped them discover and cultivate.[147]

Endeavoring to summarize the key characteristics of Greenleaf's beliefs about servant leadership, Spears provides the following list of ten characteristics:

1. Listening receptively to what others have to say.

2. Accepting others and having empathy for them.

3. Having foresight and intuition.

4. Having awareness and perception.

5. Having highly developed powers of persuasion.

6. Having an ability to conceptualize and to communicate concepts.

7. Having an ability to exert a healing influence on individuals and institutions.

8. Building community in the workplace.

9. Practicing the art of contemplation.

10. Recognizing that servant leadership begins with a desire to change oneself. Once that process has begun, it then becomes possible to practice servant leadership at an institutional level.[148]

Heidebrecht, writing from a Christian leader's perspective, suggests that servant leadership has three characteristics: (1) Identity. The servant leader knows who he or she is as a follower of Jesus. (2) Vision. The servant leader sees as God sees and empowers leaders to lead as God would lead. (3) Community. The servant leader leads an institution in a visionary community which is following God.[149] Servant leadership, then, is empowering people with both vision and authority for accomplishing the tasks at hand.

Millard understands servant leadership as "a philosophy and approach to leadership...a way of life and thinking."[150] This position rejects the notion of some that servant leadership is merely another style of leadership. Employees are not mere pawns to help the company reach its goals, but individuals to be served and nurtured. So servant leaders *are* servants. The characteristics of servant leadership are exemplified in their lives because these servant features are congruent with their own intrinsic values.[151] Millard has identified several traits of servant leadership:

Teamwork. The leader is a part of the whole rather than being apart from the whole.

Setting an example. The leader models behavior rather than imposing behavior.

Affirmation—The leader builds people up rather than holding them down.

Familiarity. The leader seeks to know and be known rather than seeking aloofness and insulation from those being led.

Individuality. The leader values uniqueness and differences rather than conformity.

Flexibility. The leader believes that rules and procedures should fit the needs of the people rather than the other way around.

Healing. The leader is committed to restoration and improvement rather than requiring perfection.[152]

In addition to these qualities, Millard identifies other inner qualities of the servant leader: compassion, openness, the willingness to sacrifice, and unpretentiousness.

Unique Aspects of Servant Leaders

Shawchuck explains that the world's patterns for leadership have become intolerable. Authoritarian models are challenged throughout the world. Leadership patterns of dictating, controlling, and bossing must give way to Jesus' model of serving. Such leadership is for the people, not the leader. Servant leaders are first trusted and then followed as they lead.[153]

Rinehart writes of the paradox of servant leadership. He views the servant leader as one who turns himself or herself away from empire building into selflessly serving others and making them heroes.[154] Burns is very close to the heart of a servant leader when he speaks of ideological leadership. Ideological leaders have personal needs of self-esteem and actualization like others, but also embody collective goals that equally relate to the wants, needs, and aspirations of others. The purposes of the movement or organization are held in higher esteem than their own while the need for relationship with others in the organization outweighs the need for a personal quest.[155]

Self-giving leadership is the product of an understanding of the heart of the Master Servant. Leaders are servants, not masters. Servant leaders do not see themselves as bosses, but facilitators. They instruct, guide, help, make plans, and organize workers.[156] Jesus taught the salient features of leadership by His example. He came to serve others. He gave himself to menial servant like tasks that characterized the heart of a true caring shepherd. He led in this manner and fully expected others to do the same.[157] Biblical servants do not shirk from any responsibility, even when the task leads to service in the public arena. Christ commanded His servants to be salt; that is, they are to permeate every area of society. The command to be salt denotes an active interface with a hurting and desperate world.[158]

Many leaders face the temptation to listen on the run with little intention to take seriously made suggestions or ideas too far. Kiechel, considering servant leader issues in the corporate world, encourages the kind of listening that sometimes goes against corporate trends and takes time to focus on comments and suggestions, allowing others to become part of a shared vision. This kind of leader sees himself or herself as a steward who takes seriously the work and ideas of those he or she serves.[159]

Roberts identifies a number of servant-leader characteristics among which the idea that the servant leader serves openly, authentically, and honestly with those who follow. Leadership is not a position but an attitude that manifests itself in complete vulnerability that refuses to use self-protection methods that could become counterproductive to serving others.[160] Richards submits that a servant leader will still maintain high levels of acceptance among those led, even after personal shortcomings. The vulnerable leader does in fact, through lack of presumption and a genuine sense of humility, open channels for followers to share their doubts, fears, joys, and successes. There will be a give-and-take attitude in all relationships and freedom to be oneself no matter who is around.[161]

Servant leaders are asked to enter the unfamiliar territory of operating from a basis of weakness and opposite of the world's notion that leaders are most effective when conducting business from a position of strength. The biblical servant abdicates the need to impress others and leads in a manner that runs the risk of ridicule and misunderstanding.[162] Brown argues that servant leadership is a critical aspect of balance in the life of the leader. Jesus' revolutionary message to lead from the bottom up (Mark 10:44) affronts a class-conscience culture, where privilege and position are entrenched, but lessens the risk of making the acquisition and use of leadership power an end in itself.[163]

Nouwen catches the beauty and power of the humble servant leader when he reflects on Jesus' words to Peter (John 21:18). The servant leader, like an aging individual who has lost youth and independence, must be willing to go where he or she would rather not go—to unknown, undesirable, painful places.

> The way of the Christian leader is not the way of upward mobility in which our world has invested so much, but the way of downward mobility ending on the cross. This might sound morbid and masochistic, but for those who have heard the voice of the first love and said yes to it, the downward-moving way of Jesus is the way to the joy and peace of God, a joyful peace that is not of this world.[164]

Kouzes and Posner have considered leadership from the position of what works within the real and varied contexts of leadership. They have concluded that most of what we call leadership is a myth.[165] Specifically, they refute the myth that the leader is the one with all the answers and the natural compulsion toward the great man theories that emerge from power and control issues. They affirm that leaders must be learners; they accept the reality that they don't know it all. Trust is more apt to grow in an atmosphere where limitations and weaknesses are acknowledged.[166] Trust is built when leaders make themselves vulnerable to others and do not seek to control but to support and enable, leading to the fulfillment of potential in the lives of those who follow.[167]

Servant leadership does militate against the improper use of power. Greenleaf sees power as a means of discharging CEO responsibilities through a wide range of strategies.

The CEO enjoys using power to get other people's power turned to support what he or she wants to do.

The CEO uses power to know more, and in a wider perspective, than those whose power the CEO needs to bend to support his or her goals.

The CEO uses power to be heard.

The CEO uses power to build stronger people.

The CEO who wants to build a strong company will want all forces he or she contends with to be strong.[168]

On Becoming a Servant Leader

Assuming the servant role does not necessitate that one forfeit the power and authority to lead an organization Wagner cites the apostle Paul as an example of the individual who viewed himself as a servant of Christ and at the same time insisted on his authority as an apostle (Rom. 1:1; 1 Cor. 4:16; 11:1).[169] Richards notes that in many successful congregations the pastor is viewed as a strong, authoritative individual to whom people joyfully submit in sincere and dedicated service. The conclusion is that such leaders learn how to combine humility with power and servanthood with leadership.[170]

For the servant leader, acquiring personal power yields to the higher call of empowering and enabling others. Jesus' strategy was to empower His disciples to become servants of God, witnesses to the world, and servants to one another (Acts 1:8). The contemporary church must take its cue from the Master Servant and also understand what many contemporary organizations intuitively know: visionary leadership welcomes the empowerment of people through learning that awakens experimentation, entrepreneurialism, and widespread participation within the ranks.[171] The striking effectiveness of learning organizations led Senge to observe that such organizations will truly excel in the future by tapping people's commitment and capacity to learn at all levels in the organization.[172] Hesselbein, Goldsmith, and Beckhard believe that the serving leader recognizes the dignity and worth of all people as divinely created beings. Leaders, therefore, involve themselves in the process of creating the work environment in which individuals can grow and flourish, discovering their potential as happy and wholesome individuals.[173]

Servant Leadership and Church Renewal

Schwarz's significant study of five thousand churches worldwide led to some amazing, if not provocative conclusions. Isolating eight characteristics of growing and revitalized churches, he postulates that small holistic groups that are trained to serve and care for one another are essential to church growth. Such groups are designed to transfer life through service to one another, not rote learning of abstract concepts.[174] Turner's personal journey into servanthood convinced him that the leader contributes to the personal renewal of individuals when he or she releases people into a loving atmosphere that enables the "reborn" leader to turn traditions upside down so that congregations can experience self-discovery and the freedom to be and become.[175]

Servant leadership and its companion concepts of individual responsibility and corporate renewal are successfully wed together when laity understands the responsibility of carrying out pastoral ministry to the Church and world at large. Each individual has his or her own "little flock of God" with which one interfaces in ordinary life. The practical consequence of understanding that each individual has the responsibility of pastoring the world is that Christians treat people—in and out of church—as if they were God's flock, recognizing that every individual represents an occasion to demonstrate God's love through service. This is shepherding miniaturized, and represents a potential extension of servant leadership that goes far beyond the ability of trained pastoral professionals who can address only a small part of the social and spiritual pain of society.[176]

Snyder attempts to answer the tough questions of societal and church revitalization within a secular culture by postulating that the reign of God can be extended throughout the world when the Church accepts responsibility for moving the kingdom of God forward through practical programs of ministry that establish and maintain kingdom principles as the center of ministry effort. He cites sixteen kingdom principles that are vital to successfully bring the reign of God to earth and calls for plural or shared pastoral leadership and the Christian ministry as a stewardship committed to all believers. He contends that the church's life and theology must be based in a real serving community with a balance of worship and evangelism.[177] Similarly, Weatherhead had argued decades before that the Church would experience the life and power of the kingdom of God only as the Church deals with its lovelessness and embraces the creed of kindness that translates into a concern for and deeds to the needy and forgotten.[178]

Young makes a case for prayer as the basis for renewal in the Church. So-called renewal teams must examine their own motives and work out a continuing personal renewal plan for individual restoration and growth through prayer. God must be sought, His leading discovered.[179] An abundance of spiritual life awaits those who are deeply in love with Jesus and forsake dreams of personal power and success. The way of the Christian leader is not upward mobility, but the way of downward mobility that ends at the Cross.[180]

Parish and Sproul advocate the development of Key Covenant Teams that accept the ongoing responsibility of church renewal. An important part of this strategy is the aspect of covenant that commits individuals to an active development of spiritual ministry competencies in themselves and others. Equipped individuals bear godly fruit as they in turn serve and equip others.[181]

The concept of servant evangelism has emerged in certain churches that wish to reach communities through institutional servanthood. These churches want God's love embodied in practical generosity and kindness. This is viewed as a "low risk, high grace" approach that is attractive to those outside the church.[182] Dempster, explaining the churches' "diakonic ministry," believes that various community ministries constitute these churches' diakonic ministry. He teaches that those touched by the gospel of the Kingdom will cultivate both an awareness and response to the poor, hungry, sick, and generally deprived individuals.[183]

Leadership has a keen responsibility to lead people into the serving and loving experience of community. It is in community that pride and hypocrisy fall before the disciplinary gaze of caring individuals.[184] Miller advocates the need for servant leaders to bring followers into community oneness. This sense of community contributes to job satisfaction and personal security. Community is the place where the servant leader suffuses followers with his or her ideals.[185] Community is a place of safety and spiritual renewal. True community plunges into the messy world of relationships and calls on its citizens to admit their failures, to identify tensions, and to explore shortcomings.[186]

The leadership patterns of the world cannot provide for the spiritual and numerical revitalization needed in the contemporary church. The prevailing pattern of worldly leadership is to control, to dictate, to boss. Jesus' word to the authoritarian patterns is clear: "It shall not be so among you." Even the people of the world understand the inadequacy of the old paradigm that champions authoritarian patterns of leadership. People want more ownership through empowerment for participation. This mood should not worry church leaders. Servant leadership emerges as a primary characteristic of the leader who understands that at the heart of congregational renewal is the desire to serve and then lead. He or she lives to serve the people. Such a leader will never be short of followers who are committed to the tasks at hand. People will always respond to a leader who is first proven and trusted as a servant.[187]

Chapter 4
STRATEGIES FOR THE 21ST CENTURY

This project was developed around the concept that servant leadership is a vital and accurate expression of biblical leadership. It is in the spirit and dynamic of the biblical model of servant leadership that contemporary leaders can expect to flourish and sustain significant advances for God's kingdom within current world cultures. Since the scriptural message and methodologies for leadership are instructive, recapturing them in the modern church is desirable and essential.

At the heart of the project was an instructional effort aimed at developing the servant leader model at the pastoral level. A seminar in servant leadership was conducted for those pastors participating in the project. Although the effort focused upon the official pastor(s) of the local church, other key church leaders within the assembly were invited to attend. The training components of the project included a series of lectures and discussions more fully described in the following sections.

Preliminary Inquiries

After conferring with the district superintendents of the North Dakota and Montana Districts of the Assemblies of God, permission was given to extend an invitation to all active pastors and interested laypeople within these districts to participate in the project. The district superintendents responded favorably to the plan and demonstrated an authentic enthusiasm for the topic of servant leadership. The initial invitation to participate in the study was sent to all the active pastors of the North Dakota and Montana districts for a total of 143 pastors (see appendix 1). The initial invitation contained a response device that allowed pastors to participate on one of two levels. Level one represented participation through attending the seminar and then becoming a part of the study. Level two indicated an interest in attending the seminar with no participation in the study (see appendix 2). Initially, twenty-five pastors from both districts responded to the invitation to attend. Eighteen pastors from North Dakota and seven from Montana elected to be active in the project (see appendix 3).

The Instrument and Its Administration

Approximately one month before the servant leadership training seminars, an assessment instrument was sent to participating pastors. The instrument was sent to eighteen pastors in the North Dakota district and seven pastors in the Montana district. Each pastor received ten questionnaires. The instrument was to be administered in a pretest and posttest configuration to all full-time and volunteer pastors in the church and other significant heads of ministry such as members of the board and/or department heads. Since board members usually constitute a "first line" of leadership contact for the pastor, it was encouraged that any official or advisory board members be utilized in completing the questionnaires. The pretest was given approximately one month before the training seminars were offered and the posttest was administered at the end of the application of specific servant leader strategies that were developed immediately following the servant leadership seminar. The period between the pretest and the posttest was approximately ninety to one hundred days. During the time period between the pretest and posttest, servant leadership strategies developed immediately after the seminar were put in place with the expectation that an increase in the perception of servant leadership qualities, attitudes, and practices within the local church would be evident.

It should be observed that the instructor of the seminars indicated that the relatively short period of time for implementing servant leader strategies would provide only marginal time for any servant strategies to have a positive impact upon the local church. Consequently, seeing scores with marginal or no positive increases at the end of the intervention period was something that could be expected. Based upon the possibility of minimal variations in pretest and posttest scores, participants were encouraged to be aware of other values that gave merit to the effort. Developing strategies which could be useful beyond the project, implementing strategies for even the shortest periods of time, and educating a congregation to the idea that progress begins with an increased awareness of servant principles were all presented as worthy ends in themselves, irrespective of testing results.

The instrument used to collect data is the Organizational Leadership Assessment (OLA) by Dr. James Laub (see appendix 4). This is a sixty-six item instrument that has been field-tested by 828 respondents from 41 different organizations with a subsequent reliability factor of .98. The instrument was designed to reflect an individual's perception, agreement or disagreement, as to whether certain characteristics of servant leadership were being displayed within the church and within the lives of its leaders. Among the broad categories examined by the instrument, valuing and developing people was included. Specific areas measured in order to assess leaderships' ability to value and develop people included how deeply leadership believes in their people and the opportunities provided by leadership for the development and growth of those in the institution. Other pertinent values reflected in the questionnaire include building community through strong relationships, displaying authenticity through openness and accountability to others, and providing leadership through personal initiative and goal clarifications. A final critical aspect measured by the instrument focused on the question of shared leadership. Sharing power, releasing control, and promoting others are among the characteristics measured in this area. (A chart illustrating these vital areas of inquiry can be seen in appendix 5.)

Data from the instrument is typically generated by three primary groups of people including the leadership, management, and work force of the institution. The author of this project spoke with Dr. James Laub, author of the questionnaire, and confirmed that the leadership, management, and workforce categories respond well to pastors, elders/deacons, and laity. Permission was given by Dr. Laub to utilize the instrument for this project and to make a few stylistic changes in the introductory part of the instrument for the purposes of the study. Each participating pastor received ten Organization Leadership Assessment instruments. These were distributed to other key leaders in the church. The final testing group included the senior pastor and any other paid or volunteer pastor(s), the board of deacons and/or advisers. If any questionnaires remained, they were given to other high-profile leaders in the church of the pastor's choice.

Pastors and other participants were assured that the data gathered from OLA would remain highly confidential. Following the posttest phase of the project, the tabulated data was returned to the senior pastor who had the option of sharing the material with his or her leaders. It was strongly recommended in the training sessions that the posttest data be presented to the leadership of the church that completed the assessment tool in the pretest and posttest mode. It seemed logical that the data from the instrument could be helpful in assessing both strengths and weaknesses of specific servant areas within participating churches.

The Seminar

The initial phase of the project was a training seminar that could serve as a basis for the development of servant leadership attitudes and behaviors within senior pastors and key church leaders. Generally speaking, the seminar was designed to correspond to the specific areas addressed through the OLA. Specifically, the training module was designed to develop individual and institutional pastoral characteristics that value people by listening receptively, serving the needs of others first, developing people by providing innovative and biblically centered opportunities for learning, and building community through strategies that incorporate collaborative work. Other significant values incorporated in the training included displaying authenticity by raising levels of integrity and trust, providing leadership by developing a compelling and visionary future, and sharing leadership by creating shared vision and collective decision making.

Training seminars for servant leadership were conducted for volunteer pastors from the North Dakota District of the Assemblies of God and the Montana District of the Assemblies of God. Participating pastors attended five training sessions with each session lasting sixty to ninety minutes. An important aspect of the seminar presentations included open discussions that assisted the instructor and the participants in evaluating prevailing church cultures within their local churches. The focus of these discussions centered largely upon the pastoral perception of the present condition of his or her pastorate as it related to specific servant leadership characteristics as described by the instructor. Participants were encouraged to think about the demonstration of servant leader qualities in personal pastoral ministry as well as servant characteristics and practices within the church itself. Discussions were intentionally focused upon the presence or absence of servant leadership characteristics in the local church culture.

The seminar incorporated approximately six to seven hours of study on vital topics related to servant leadership. As previously stated, the content of the seminars underscored the key servant leadership characteristics stated above and inventoried by the OLA. Specific content consisted of five lectures, which provided for approximately six to seven hours of lectured material. The broad topics of the seminar and the order of their presentation were as follows: Definitions and a Short History of Servant Leadership; Characteristics and Values of Servant Leadership; Jesus and Servant Leadership; The Primitive Church, Paul and Servant Leadership; The Church as Servant; Holistic Leadership—The Leader as Servant, Steward, and Shepherd.

Each class period was structured around a strong lecturing component with adequate time for discussion along with a period of time for questions and answers at the end of each session. Lectures included a PowerPoint presentation for each of the major lessons. Participants were given workbooks developed by the instructor and followed the flow of the lecture series. The workbooks utilized the main outline of the seminar topics and allowed students to fill in missing phrases or words from the major outline. The PowerPoint presentation corresponded to the format of the workbook. The classroom environment also included normal teaching components including the liberal use of a whiteboard and overhead projector. The speaker allowed adequate time for interaction during the lecture itself.

Following the lectures, students were allowed to set up a personal time with the instructor for the purpose of discussing intervention strategies that were required after the sessions. The strategies employed focused upon the development of personal pastoral servant leadership characteristics and the development of servant leadership strategies for the church. Conversations between presenter and pastoral leaders were generally for a period of one hour, or longer if needed. Private sessions with individual pastors took place after the regular sessions were completed. Conversations centered upon prevailing local church conditions and an initial appraisal of any servant leadership strategies that could be implemented within a given local church. Future assistance was offered by the instructor for the purpose of assisting individual pastors in the development of personal and church servanthood strategies. Such help was offered through phone calls, E-mail, and regular mail.

Personal and Church Strategies

Following the sessions, pastors were encouraged to submit a servant leadership strategy for developing personal servant leadership habits and characteristics in their own lives. Such strategies might include personal prayer focusing upon cultivating a deep humility and growing love for others, acceleration in deeds of kindness for others, and individual efforts to serve other church leaders. These and other practical strategies were among the several ideas discussed for personal servant skills development.

The importance of providing a servant leadership example for the church was emphasized. Pastors were encouraged to think about strategies that would help develop a servant lifestyle that would perpetuate itself beyond the study and last for a lifetime of ministry. While it was acknowledged that various personal strategies would be developed for the purpose of the study, it was more important to take ownership of the need for pastoral servanthood as a permanent ministry style. The study served as an introduction to a more effective way for doing church and carrying out meaningful pastoral ministry.

Additionally, pastors were encouraged to develop servant leadership strategies for their churches. These strategies were to include the senior pastoral leadership training of other pastoral and key lay leaders in personal servanthood attitudes, habits, and techniques. Strong encouragement was given to organizing a small training seminar for significant church leaders who could assist in putting servant leadership strategies in place as a vital component of the project. An emphasis was placed upon developing in-church strategies that were compassionate and authentic in their expression. A basic guideline for developing strategies was given to the seminar participants (see appendix 6). Leaders were encouraged to do everything possible to avoid any perception that planned servant leadership strategies were mere mechanical devices put in place in order to create the appearance of a serving church.

During the training sessions, significant time was given to discussion that included practical suggestions and ideas for servant leader expressions and practices. A number of interesting, if not creative, approaches came into focus during these discussion times. It appeared that participants in the seminar understood the desire of the instructor to develop strategies of servanthood that would address the practical and spiritual needs of the individuals within the church. These strategies would simultaneously serve as a means of raising the awareness of the servant attitude within the congregation.

Armed with the information from the seminar, participants were to return to their home churches and recruit high-profile church leadership for the purpose of training them in basic servant leadership strategies. When those already in a high-profile position would begin to practice servant leadership in its various forms, others in the church could be challenged by their example.

The phrase "first-line leaders" was used for these high- profile leaders. The training of first-line leaders was compared to Jesus' training of his twelve disciples and then commissioning them to go forward in the spirit of servanthood (Luke 22:24-28). First-line leaders would minister to others and through example would encourage and train others to become servants also.

The following guidelines were given for the development of servant leader strategies within participating churches:

The strategy should be relatively simple. As much emphasis would be placed upon the practice of the attitudes of servant-hood as was the acts or strategies themselves.

Rather than to depend upon one strategy to carry the day, it was encouraged that two or three different strategies be working at the same time. For example, the pastor could begin to develop servant leader attitudes and expressions that were closely tied to his or her own pastoral ministry. At the same time, board members could be encouraged to display servant attitudes through a specific ministry with practical applications, that is, making hospital calls or visiting a sick parishioner.

It was important for the pastor to develop a plan of action for his or her own efforts in servant leadership. This personal strategy was to be implemented irrespective of what other strategies may or may not have been developed. As in all matters of leadership, the leader must lead the leaders!

Strategies would have a sixty-day to ninety-day duration during which initial training in servant leadership principles and the implementation of given strategies would take place.

Initial strategies would be viewed as an introduction to a greater life of service to the kingdom of God. Servant leadership could not be a short-term proposition. These initial strategies would be the beginning of a new day of service within the local church. In terms of service, better things could be expected for the future.

Servant projects and strategies were submitted to the instructor in written form and could be as simple as desired. In fact, simplicity was encouraged. Because of the relatively brief period of time available for developing, applying, and measuring the effectiveness of a given strategy, participants were encouraged to develop strategies that could be perpetuated after the study was concluded. Students were made aware of the fact that the brevity of the study would allow strategies to have only marginal time for effectiveness. The instructor emphasized that while the pretest and posttest configuration might indicate a rise in the perception of servant leadership qualities after the application of the servant leader strategies, the relatively short length of the application of any interventions could fail to show any positive perception or awareness of servant leadership principles and qualities. It was emphasized that the most important value of the project was key church leaders beginning to serve Christ and His church in a manner consistent with biblical servanthood. This alone should be viewed as a major benefit of the study. Perpetuating servant leadership attitudes, practices, and expressions over the long haul of ministry would be the ultimate goal of the study.

Summarily, the project and intervention consisted of the three components: (1) a pretest and posttest configuration, (2) a training seminar in servant leadership concepts and strategies, and (3) a practical application of servant leadership strategies within the church. Another important aspect of the project was an evaluation of the seminar by participating students (see appendix 7) and an evaluation of the entire project by the senior pastor (see appendix 8). Data was gathered in three essential areas: (1) the OLA assessment tool, (2) class evaluations, and (3) pastoral evaluation of the overall project. (These data are given under the evaluation section of the project in chapter 6.

The following training objectives and concerns drove the research model used in this project. The design of the project focused upon the senior pastor as the key for learning, developing, and integrating important servant leadership principles into the corporate life of the church. Intervention strategies rested on the shoulders of the pastoral leaders who should most naturally be expressing the servant attitudes that ideally characterize all churches.

At the very least, the OLA introduced the idea of quantifying perceived realities within a local church. Several of the pastors participating had never experienced the idea of allowing others to quantify their perceptions of certain issues or needs in the church. The speaker encouraged pastors to become comfortable with an attitude of inquiry throughout a lifetime of ministry. A natural feeling of vulnerability should not keep a caring pastor from discovering if others feel his or her efforts are effective. Growing leaders were encouraged to become comfortable with the ideas of risk and inquiry. During the process of introducing the OLA, an effort was made to present the use of inventories and research instruments as a valid means for assisting leadership in the continual pursuit and development of people-oriented ministries and programs of excellence.

Another priority of the research design was to demonstrate the value of interaction with other pastors and church leaders facing similar issues in church growth and congregational indifference to human need. Seminar sessions were typically honest and open. Participants were encouraged to take hard objective looks at their ministry style and how well it was working within the church. This level of honesty often leads to self-discovery and subsequent commitment to a servant life-style that focuses upon human need.

The training approach also endeavored to create a heightened sense of inquiry into the vast amount of servant leadership literature available to church leadership. During the sessions, the speaker made over forty book titles available for a cursory inspection by those who attended the seminars. A bibliography was also shared with each participant. The bibliography included authors from a Christian philosophy of servant leadership as well as writers from organizational and leadership schools of thought. Those with Internet resources were given pertinent e-mail addresses that focused upon leadership in general and servant leadership specifically.

It was desired that the basic principles of servant leadership would "catch fire" and the participants would return home to share the basic principles and methods of the seminar with their congregation and other pastoral leadership. Therefore, the training included the elementary principles of servant leadership from both Christian and organizational perspectives. A strong emphasis was placed upon the need to train key leaders in the same principles and methods shared in the seminar and, subsequently, develop local church methodologies based upon the important servant teachings of Scripture. Students were encouraged to use any of the materials developed and presented by the instructor during the seminars. All sessions were taped and some students acquired a full set of the seminar tapes to assist in their training efforts in the local church.

An important aspect of the project included continual contact with those participating in the project. A series of letters kept the project leader in contact with the participants. The letters were often accompanied by selected articles on servant leadership. A total of seven letters were written during the weeks following the training sessions. E-mails were commonly exchanged, while others chose to dialogue by telephone. When requested by the participants, the instructor gave personal guidance in project development and application.

Chapter 5
DESCRIPTION OF A SERVANT PROJECT

District Contact

The initial step of the project was to contact district superintendents of the Montana and North Dakota Districts of the Assemblies of God. Reverend Paul Goodman of the Montana District Council of the Assemblies of God and Reverend Leon Freitag of the North Dakota District of the Assemblies of God were contacted by telephone in mid- March 2000. A conversation explaining the nature and design of the project was shared. Each superintendent expressed a high level of interest in allowing pastors from their respective districts participate in the study.

Interestingly, both superintendents conveyed similar concerns about the "testing" aspect of the project. One superintendent demonstrated concern that if he became personally aware of the testing results then participating pastors might feel personally threatened by his firsthand knowledge of the perceived health of their churches as revealed through the testing procedure. It was agreed that it would be advisable to let the pastors know that the information would be entirely confidential and not released to anyone except the participating pastor. It would then be at the discretion of the pastor to share the information with his or her district leadership.

The other superintendent shared a similar concern that participating pastors might feel threatened if the testing conveyed overwhelmingly negative perceptions by those filling out the questionnaires. While it could not be denied that this possibility existed, the general response was that pastors in that situation would have to mentally and spiritually prepare themselves for test scores lower than their expectations. Furthermore, a point was made that in some cases pastors could possible use a reality check concerning how others felt regarding the health of the general ministries of the church. Both superintendents were informed that during the seminar the instructor would take time to encourage pastors to be fair-minded about the results and further understand that responses are often subjective in nature and may or may not depict reality. It would also be emphasized that some form of measuring the perceived efficiency of leadership can be a healthy, ongoing practice in the pastoral ministries.

In the end, both superintendents were comfortable with the safeguards that would protect the interest of their leadership, the pastors participating, and the relationships in their local churches. Each superintendent expressed a high level of enthusiasm for the project, and both immediately loaned support to the effort by writing their pastors and encouraging them to become involved in the training seminars and study aspects of the program.

Superintendent Paul Goodman agreed that the seminar could be conducted with his pastors during the Family Camp, July 3-7, 2000. Superintendent Leon Freitag confirmed that two training sessions would be given in his district. Seminar one would be given in Jamestown, North Dakota, on June 6, 2000. Seminar two would be given in Bismarck, North Dakota, on June 8, 2000. Each of these seminars would begin at 1:00 p.m. and conclude at 6:30 p.m. the same evening. The same seminar would be given in two locations and would serve to accommodate pastors from the eastern and western parts of the state of North Dakota.

Participant Invitation

After clearance with the district superintendents, invitations for participation were sent during the first two weeks of April, 2000 to all of the active pastors of each district (see appendix 1). Pertinent information concerning dates, location, and intent of the study was given. The important aspects of the study were also outlined and general benefits for participation in the study were presented. A simple return device was included with a return envelope that allowed for pastors to participate on one of two levels (see appendix 2). Level one included participation in the study following the seminar. Those participating on this level would receive two hours of college credit (CA320) with Trinity Bible College of Ellendale, North Dakota, upon their completion of the entire study. Credit would be awarded if participants became responsible for distributing the questionnaire in the pretest phase of the study. Additionally, the seminar had to be attended and then the posttest distributed to the same individuals who completed the pretest. The posttest would then be returned to the instructor for evaluation. Level two involved only attending the seminar.

Following the mailing of the first invitation, a second invitation was sent during the first week of May, 2000 to all active pastors in both districts. Again, this brief invitation included the pertinent information of purpose, date, time, and location of the seminar.

Questionnaire Mailing (Pretest)

Upon the receipt of the individual confirmations indicating an interest in the study, a letter expressing appreciation for participation in the study was sent (see appendix 9). These letters were typically mailed out within twenty-four hours of receiving the returned response device. This letter informed the participant that over the next few days ten Organizational Leadership Assessments would arrive and should be distributed and completed according to the instructions contained in the pretest packet. The same letter briefly reiterated the pretest-posttest approach to the study.

During the balance of the month of May, the Organizational Leadership Assessments were sent to pastors indicating an interest in the study. Twenty-five sets (250 questionnaires) were sent to pastors in North Dakota and fifteen sets (150 questionnaires) were sent to pastors in Montana. These questionnaires were accompanied by a letter providing general instructions for their distribution, completion, and return (see appendix 10). Additional general instructions and questionnaire description were also part of the introductory material on the questionnaire itself. The intent was to have the pretest completed and returned by the time pastors attended the respective seminars.

North Dakota Seminars

Seminar one was held in Jamestown, North Dakota, on June 6, 2000. Although the seminar was scheduled to go through 6:30 p.m., the seminar concluded at approximately 7:30 p.m. Twenty-five people attended the seminars. Two of the students were lay individuals, three students were pastors' wives, and the rest were male pastors in active ministry.

Seminar two was held in Bismarck, North Dakota, on June 8, 2000. Although the seminar was scheduled to go through 6:30 p.m., the seminar extended through 7:30 p.m. Eighteen people attended the seminar, including the district superintendent of the North Dakota district. All of the students were pastors or associate pastors. There were no female pastors or pastors' wives present.

Montana Seminar

The third seminar was held during the Family Camp of the Montana District Council of the Assemblies of God, July 3-7, 2000, at Glacier Park Campground in Hungry Horse, Montana. One-hour sessions were held daily in the camp chapel from 9:00-10:30 a.m. The number of those attending changed from day to day, but approximately twelve pastors and three to four pastors' wives attended daily with the intention of being a part of the complete study. The average attendance for each session was thirty-five individuals that included pastors, interested lay individuals, and district leaders.

At the end of each seminar in the North Dakota locations and the Montana location, participants were asked to evaluate the overall study. They were queried in such areas as effectiveness of presentation by the instructor, relevance of material, professionalism and enthusiasm of the instructor, and other vital areas of the seminar presentation.

Strategy Development

An important aspect of the project was the two weeks following the seminar. During this period of time pastors were requested to develop a servant ministry strategy that would serve two fundamental purposes: (1) The development of servant ministry strategies would raise both the pastors' and church's level of awareness concerning the value, need, and expression of servant attitudes and ministries. (2) Servant ministries and servant leadership within the congregation and community would minister to the practical and spiritual needs of individuals.

Those choosing to develop a strategy after returning home were requested to have a written strategy completed and returned to the instructor within the two weeks following the seminar. A letter encouraging the development of a strategy was sent within two or three days after each seminar (see appendix 11). Included with this letter was a bibliography on servant leadership texts and a helpful servant leadership article. A second letter encouraging a written and filed strategy was sent on August 1, 2000, to those who still indicated a desire to be a part of the study but had not filed a strategy (see appendix 12). An enlightening article on servant leadership and pastoral ministry was sent with this letter. Although filing a strategy was optional to participating in the study, a total of thirteen pastors from both districts chose to work from a written strategy.

Those not filing a specific strategy were encouraged to preach or teach occasionally on the topic of servanthood and endeavor to more consistently display attitudes of pastoral servanthood within the context of their ministries. They were not asked to document what they had done. They too would be asked to do the posttest at the end of the study.

Strategy Implementation

The instructor encouraged students to communicate via regular mail, E-mail, or telephone as they implemented servanthood strategies. Initially, the study was to end by October 15, 2000. Later, the date was extended to November 15, 2000, in order to give additional time for the positive impact of the strategies. Near the end of September another written communication to the participants informed them of the additional time to work strategies and the extended deadline for returning questionnaires (see appendix 13). Another article related to servant leadership was sent with this correspondence.

Pastoral Questionnaire and Posttest

Included with the September letter was the Pastoral Questionnaire that was designed to help appraise the participating pastor's overall response to the project (see appendix 8). Pastoral responses to the project would also be a vital part of the assessment and evaluation process at the end of the study. Pastors were requested to return the questionnaire by the end of October.

Copies of the Organizational Leadership Assessment were also sent with this mailing. Completing the OLA constituted the posttest phase of the study. Questionnaires were to be returned by November 15, 2000.

Evaluation and Conclusions

The month of December was given to reviewing the Organizational Leadership

Assessment and the Pastoral Questionnaire. This discussion constitutes the final chapter of the project.

Chapter 6
SUMMARY AND EVALUATION

Pastoral Questionnaire—Categories of Inquiry

The Pastoral Servant Leadership Questionnaire (see appendix 8) was used to assess the perceived overall effectiveness of the leadership strategies designed and applied by the pastors participating in the project. The applied strategies are referred to as "projects" in the questionnaire. The questionnaire specifically addresses those unique strategies developed by each pastor for his or her church. The questionnaire contained eighteen questions that have been grouped into the following general categories with their respective subdivisions: the strategy's impact upon the personal life and ministry of the participating pastor, the strategy's impact upon church life and ministry, the general awareness of servanthood in the church, future planning, and vision for the local church.

The strategy's impact upon personal life and ministry was queried through questions 3, 4, 8, and 11. The strategy's impact upon church life and ministry was queried through questions 5, 6, 7, 9, 14, 15, 16, 17, and 18. The strategy's impact upon vision and future planning included questions 10, 12, and 13. The general awareness of servant leadership strategies was queried through questions 1 and 2.

Thirteen Pastoral Servant Leadership Questionnaires and one letter from each of the participating pastors generally describing the pastor's overall impression of the effectiveness of his or her strategies were returned before the required deadline. Two pastors indicated their strategies were begun late and the completion of the questionnaires evaluating the study could not be filled out by the required deadlines.

The General Awareness of the Servant Leader Strategies

A significant heightened awareness of servanthood attitudes and actions in the church and in the personal life of the participating pastor was targeted in this area. After the strategies were applied in each of the participating churches, 75 percent of the responding pastors indicated a general increased awareness of servanthood on a congregational level. One pastor indicated an increased congregational awareness of servanthood activities and attitudes, but it was not considered a significant awareness. Two pastors indicated no significant awareness of servanthood attitudes and activities was accomplished on the church level. It appears that those who saw no increase of awareness in servanthood within their congregations encountered an initial difficulty in recruiting and engaging individuals in the planned servanthood strategies. On a personal level, all pastors indicated an increased awareness of servanthood attitudes and activities in the church.

Strategies' Impact Upon Personal Life and Ministry

Long Range Efforts

Ninety-two percent of the pastors responding indicated a deeper commitment to personal servanthood and the development and implementation of long- term servant leadership projects within their churches.

Relationships

Participating pastors seem to enjoy a wide range of personal benefits associated with the study. Twenty-five percent of those participating directly linked improved relationships with members of the congregation as a benefit of their applied strategies. As a product of their efforts, 16 percent of those responding seem to recognize a need to begin building better relationships within the church. Sensing a deeper love for those in the church was a benefit for 16 percent of those in the project.

Better Servants, Better Leaders

Fifty percent of those participating expressed that the applied strategies lead them to a deeper understanding of what it means to be a servant to their churches. One pastor indicated the effort had revolutionized his prayer life. Three pastors indicated their participation greatly heightened their awareness of too much "self" in ministry and not enough of the authentic love of Christ. Teaching and living the servant life was a concern for one-half of the pastors responding. Thirty-three percent of those responding directly acknowledged that developing and implementing servant strategies within their churches made them better leaders. "A higher sense of ministerial priorities for people has developed for me and I now feel I am a better leader," wrote one respondent. Another participant indicated the entire exercise had helped him truly understand the meaning of the words "pastor" and "shepherd."

Practical Developments

A variety of practical benefits seemed to emerge for some of those participating in the project. These benefits included a better use of time (16 percent) and an increased ability to set the right priorities in ministry. One pastor observed that with others working for others in a spirit of servanthood, there were fewer fires to put out in the church! Additionally, he stated he now had more time for his own spiritual development. Another pastor developed a new view of the practical side of ministry. "I am now a true facilitator and practitioner," he stated.

Personal Spirituality

Seventy-five percent of those participating noted the personal, spiritual benefits of developing and guiding their people into servanthood. A deepening prayer life, a greater awareness of God, a lingering sense of Christ's blessing, and a general sense of church and spiritual renewal were among the statements that appeared to convey a new emerging spirituality for participating pastors.

Impact upon Church Life and Ministry

Spiritual Welfare

Ninety two percent of the participating pastors indicated that the servant strategies benefited their churches from a spiritual standpoint. When asked to explain their response, a number of interesting and enlightening answers were given. One-third of the pastors indicated that the new focus upon others brought a greater sense of unity among the people. The practical implications of this new spiritual unity is framed by one pastor's statement: "With my people working together and focusing more upon the needs of one another, I have found there are fewer negative issues surfacing in church life."

Twenty-five percent of the churches claimed an increased commitment to prayer as a result of servant activities. One pastor reported an obvious new dependence upon the Holy Spirit as the leadership ventured into new servant activities. "Outreach," "evangelism," and "reaching the lost" were themes that emerged in 33 percent of the participating churches as a direct spiritual impact of implementing the servant strategies.

A heightened sense of God's presence was noted in 58 percent of the churches participating, although one pastor wisely noted that other factors beyond servant efforts are undoubtedly at work when there is a Spirit visitation. Twenty-five percent of the pastors felt that some members of their congregation felt a fresh awareness of God that was particularly concentrated within those who were working with the servant strategies. Two pastors indicated there was no particular change in the congregational spiritual atmosphere.

When given the opportunity to indicate some level of spiritual impact that strategies made upon individual churches, 67 percent of the respondents indicated that the strategies "had some effect upon spiritual life." Twenty-five percent indicated "a significant positive effect upon the spiritual life of the congregation," and 8 percent (one respondent) indicated that the effort had "little or no spiritual impact upon the spiritual life of his church."

From a pastoral perspective, it appears that the overall impact of servant strategies had an uplifting spiritual impact upon the participating churches. With one exception, all pastoral comments were positive in this vital area. In the cases of participating churches, it appears that the work of servants may bring churches to some basic points of spiritual awakening that incorporates increased prayer, a deeper awareness of others and their needs, and a heightened desire to reach the lost.

Church Growth

Because of the relatively short ninety-day duration allowed for the implementation of servant strategies, growth issues were downplayed in the seminar presentation. It did seem appropriate, however, to allow participating churches to indicate any growth that may have occurred during the effort. Sixty-seven percent of the churches had no growth during the ninety-day effort; 25 percent reported some growth, and one church decreased in attendance due to demographic influences, according to the pastor.

The short duration of the servant efforts may or may not have contributed to the short-term growth of three of the churches involved. There was no indication that any efforts were aimed specifically at church growth in these three churches. It should be remembered that church growth does come slowly in many parts of rural America, particularly in the upper Midwest where demographics often hinder meaningful church growth. The fact that numerical growth had taken place in three churches seemed very encouraging to the pastors involved and generally convinced them that servant efforts were at least partially responsible.

Better Servants?

A vast majority of the church leaders (83 percent) participating in servant projects within their churches seemed to grow in servanthood, according to their pastors. One pastor perceived no growth in servanthood attitudes in those participating while one pastor was not sure of any perceptible growth in his participants. The litmus test of servant leadership may be contained in Robert Greenleaf's most memorable proposition: "Do those served grow as persons; do they, while being served, become healthier, wiser, freer, more autonomous, more likely themselves to becomes servants?"[188] One would therefore expect favorable results after a servant leadership strategy has been carried out. This seemed to be the case in the majority of those participating in the project.

When responding to a similar question that asked if those participating in servant strategies became "stronger servants," the percentages were essentially the same as those in the preceding paragraph. Two pastors saw minimal growth in the attitudes of servanthood, but both were hopeful that continued teaching and modeling would continue leading their people into new dimensions of service to God's kingdom. Regarding the emergence of stronger servants, only one pastor viewed his participants in a virtual nongrowth situation following the implementation of servant strategies.

General Congregational Benefits

A primary call of the contemporary servant leader is to nurture those he or she leads in such a manner that those led are pulsating evidence of vitality that is born of servant efforts. Consequently, it should not be difficult for either the leader or the servant disciple to articulate the benefits that are inherent with the servant lifestyle. DiStefano believes that the central element of the human spirit is theological, and although this constitutes a mystery of sorts for those seeking to understand the full potential of the individual, the development of the theological center of one's self is not. A sensitive servant leader should continually enhance maturing servants through serious training efforts that produce marked benefits in the lives of those tutored in servant ways.[189]

The participants in this study seemed to bring a wide array of corporate benefits into the churches they served. Pastors observed several positive characteristics and behaviors that were consistent from one congregation to the next. Pastors saw new spiritual life emerging through rising levels of commitment to prayer and other spiritual graces. One leader remarked that the efforts of servanthood brought more of a spirit of renewal or revival into his church than any other recent effort focused upon spiritual renewal.

Twenty-five percent of the pastors recognized a new proactive approach to the practical ministry needs of the church. It seemed that many began to see opportunities for ministry that before were overlooked or disregarded. On a more abstract note, two pastors spoke of renewed vision for the future of the church.

An escalating awareness of a variety of human needs within the congregation appeared as a benefit for three of the participating churches. It appeared that those trained in simple servant methods began to see their fellows in a new way. In one case, this new awareness of needs prompted members of the congregation to continually look for new places and people to serve.

The most reoccurring theme under congregational benefits was clearly the emergence of better relationships within the cadre of those carrying out the servant ministries. Seventy-five percent of the churches participating seemed to experience a significant relational dynamic at work when servant ministries were carried out. "New and more intimate friendships were developed," "brokenness was restored," "better relationships in church," and several other similar phrases indicated a stronger bonding among those who chose to serve.

Servanthood and the Future

The original training seminars emphasized developing servant efforts that would go beyond the time limits of the applied project. All but one pastor indicated a desire to continue to research servant leadership projects for the future of their churches. The one pastor who declined was in a doctoral program and had no time to take servant effort any further in the near future. One hundred percent of the participating pastors indicated a personal desire to continue individual development of servant leader strategies and qualities within their personal ministries.

A variety of responses were given when participants were queried about any projects that were planned after the completion of the seminar projects. Three churches indicated that no specific plans had yet developed, but the process of future planning was already in place. Three churches indicated no plans were being made beyond the completion of the study project. Two churches indicated that servant leadership strategies had been incorporated into their vision for the future and planning would come accordingly. The balance of participating churches had developed a relatively small number of practical strategies for the future which included light mechanical work for those would could not otherwise afford it, carpentry work, Christmas baskets and stockings, Women's Ministries helping in a variety of ways, and a new program for welcoming guests into the church and community.

All pastors had favorable comments in all the areas addressed by the questionnaire. Only one questionnaire had an overriding negative tone. It appears that a serious lack of cooperation among the congregants lead one leader to a series of rather negative observations. A hard reality of any ministry effort is that often there will be those who for whatever reasons may not seem sufficiently responsive to make a difference.

The response of the participating pastors seemed open and honest. It did not appear that any answers were overstated. Honesty and accuracy were encouraged, and the writer feels that the spirit of the responses met these criteria.

It appears that in almost all categories, the responses were mildly to strongly positive. It would be difficult to feel that these short-term efforts fell short of the important goal of introducing servant concepts into the general congregation at the hands of the serving shepherds.

Organizational Leadership Assessment

The Organizational Leadership Assessment (see appendix 4) was used in a pretest and posttest configuration with twenty pastors initially participating in the pretest mode. After the intervention of the servant leadership strategies by local church leadership, the OLA was administered again as a posttest. Thirteen churches responded in the posttest phase of the study. The results and evaluations of those results are summarized in the following pages.

Each questionnaire was scored both in the pretest and posttest phase and then the difference between the two scores was calculated. In addition to the preceding information, scores were calculated from the three major sections of the sixty-six-item questionnaire. These areas included questions that applied to the entire organization (questions 1-21), questions that applied to the leadership of the organization (questions 22-54), and questions that applied personally to the respondent and his or her role in the organization (questions 55-66). A pretest and posttest score with the numerical difference was calculated for each of these major sections of the OLA.

Finally, the posttest evaluation included pretest and posttest scores and their numerical differences based upon the six characteristics of leadership and organizational practices critical to servant leadership. These characteristics included valuing people, developing people, building community, displaying authenticity, providing leadership, and sharing leadership. This provided each pastor with a total number of ten scores from the OLA.

Six of the thirteen churches reporting experienced a statistical increase in the six values measured by the instrument. Three churches experienced a statistical increase in five of the six values measured. One church experienced a statistical increase in four of the six values measured. Two churches experienced statistical increases in one of the six values measured. One church experienced no increases in the values measured. No churches remained exactly the same in any of the six values measured.

It appears that the servant interventions were responsible for a general increase of favorable perceptions of the six values measured. Ten of the churches reported increased statistical values in either all or no less than four of the six values measured. Only one church decreased in all of the values measured, while two churches decreased in four of the values measured.

Pastoral Report

This information was sent back to the pastors in a report form (see appendix 14 and 15) to share with those individuals who cooperated with them in the study. The report included the following suggestions as to how the information could benefit future planning and implementation of servant activities.

Make copies of the report and share the information with each person who participated in the assessment.

Identify areas in which scores fell lower than expected.

Create a safe and open dialogue on how the total organization and its leadership can improve in each of the six characteristics, particularly those which fell in the lower score ranges or those that failed to improve after the intervention.

Create a practical list of suggested improvements that will become the bedrock for an action plan that will move the church forward.

Provide training and development opportunities in any or all of the six characteristics.

Prayerfully determine to move forward in a positive way in your church leadership practices.

It was expected that the pastors would use the vital information from the OLA to help establish any perceived benefits from the short-term strategies and identify both weak and strong areas in leadership and organizational practice. The long-term benefit of the exercise and information derived from it would be a safe and open dialogue on how the local church and its pastoral leadership can improve in each of the six characteristics measured. The purpose of ongoing dialogue would be to provide a list of suggested improvements for establishing servant leadership as a way of doing church ministry over the long haul. The implications of such a list would be the development of training and development opportunities in any or all of the six characteristics. The relevant scores of the thirteen churches completing the posttest phase are given in table 1.

Table 1.

Cumulative Pretest and Posttest Averages and Differences			
	Pre	*Post*	*Diff*
Church A	3.314	4.348	1.034
Church B	3.635	4.058	0.423
Church C	4.298	4.712	0.414
Church D	3.885	4.197	0.312
Church E	3.986	4.237	0.251
Church F	3.774	3.975	0.200
Church G	3.825	3.980	0.155
Church H	3.728	3.871	0.142
Church I	3.959	4.069	0.111
Church J	4.018	4.018	0.000
Church K	4.313	4.220	-0.093
Church L	4.381	4.208	-0.173
Church M	4.687	4.386	-0.301

Nine of the participating churches demonstrated an increased score on the overall score after the intervention of the servanthood strategies. The largest increase between the pretest and posttest scores was Church A with 1.034 while the lowest increase was Church I with .111 increase. The average increase of posttest scores over pretest scores of all churches showing an increase was .338.

One church remarkably stayed the same while three churches experienced declining scores after the intervention. The largest declining score was Church M with -.301.

The preceding statistics provide a range of scores from a positive 1.034 to a negative score of -.301. The average score between pretest and posttest scores for all thirteen participating churches was .190. The median increase of all thirteen scores was .1556.

Although the results of overall increases was encouraging and seemed to indicate that the servant interventions had positive impacts in approximately 70 percent of the participating churches, the limiting factors of the study must be kept in focus. The short duration of the servant strategies is possibly the most problematic aspect of any high probability of statistical accuracy for this project. Other factors that preclude statistical certainty in this study must include the normal biases or attitudes of the participants, the quality and consistency of the servant strategies, and the small number of respondents in some cases.

On the other hand, it is likely that a positive correlation exists between the servant interventions and the elevated scores in some of the cases. Similarly, for all the same reasons stated above, it should not be assumed that scores that remained the same or went down necessarily reflect an inadequate intervention.

Sectional Scores

The Organizational Leadership Assessment is divided into three sections. These sections assess the working environment of the entire organization (questions 1-21), the leadership of the organization (questions 22-54), and general feelings of the respondent toward the institution and general job satisfaction (questions 55-66). The following data is based upon the sectional scores of the thirteen churches reporting.

A total of thirteen churches provided the following observation. Eight of the churches experienced increases of posttest averages over pretest averages in all three sections of the instrument. Three churches experienced increases in two sections and a loss in one section of the instrument. One church experienced one sectional increase with a loss in two sections. One church experienced a loss in all three sections.

An average of pretest scores for all churches revealed that the lowest scoring area was section I which measured the perceptions of servant leadership for the entire organization. Values such as trust and acceptance were measured heavily in this section. Furthermore, this was the area that had the least amount of improvement in pretest and posttest scores for all churches. For section I, the average for all churches for the pretest was 3.873. This score represented a .173 increase over the pretest averages for all thirteen churches. Since this area demonstrated the lowest posttest average for all churches and also demonstrated the least amount of increase following the intervention, two things should be considered. First, it is possible that building trust and other important congregational values in the entire organization through servant leadership could possibly be the strongest challenge awaiting the servant leader. It may also be true that short-term strategies are less effective in raising general positive impressions about servant leadership in the entire organization when compared to perception of servant leadership qualities in leadership alone.

Section 2 of the instrument, which measured perceptions of servant leadership among the leaders of the organization, reflected the middle score for all three sections with a pretest average of 4.018. Interestingly, this area showed the largest average increase for all churches with a .345 increase in the average posttest scores. This increase is significant when compared with the .173 average increases for all churches in section 1 and .216 increase for all churches in section 3. This could possibly indicate that the pastor's obvious role in raising servant leadership awareness in the church may contribute more quickly to a raised perception of the pastor as a servant leader. At the very least, this significant increase for leaders should bring a new awareness of the attention given to the working attitudes and methodologies of all those who serve in leadership within the church.

Section 3 of the instrument, measuring general job/ministry satisfaction, provided the highest average for the participating churches with a 4.089 on the pretest score. This area experienced an average .216 increase in the average of all churches following the interventions.

The overall averages could lead one to positive assumptions about the effectiveness of even short-term servant leader strategies and interventions in relatively small churches. Given the fact that 62 percent of the churches had average increases in all three sections and that 92 percent of the churches had increases in one section or more, it seems likely that the servant leadership strategies maintained a consistently positive effect upon the churches participating. It would only seem reasonable to assume that strategies that are carefully planned and orchestrated over a longer period of time would continue to provide productive results in the critical areas measured by the instrument.

Limiting Factors

The preceding evaluations, observations, and conclusions were made with the awareness that the measurements were based upon a small sampling of small rural Assemblies of God churches (an average attendance of seventy-five people), and in some cases the number of respondents in the posttest were fewer than the number of respondents in the pretest. The relatively short duration of the intervention (sixty to ninety days in all cases) was also a factor that prevented absolute assumptions based upon test results. Other limiting factors must include existing biases that could affect a respondent's answers on the questionnaire and/or prevailing attitudes within a local church setting that could impact answers given on the instrument. The quality and consistency of the servant leader interventions put in place by a pastor after returning from the seminar could not be measured in any other manner than the questionnaire itself, which may or may not be reflected in the scores taken from the instrument.

Pastoral Follow-Through

The overall impression of the scores should encourage the participating pastors to continue indefinitely into the future some kind of servant leadership strategies. Given the short duration of both the training seminar and the intervention period, the general results seem very good, enough so that pastors should take seriously the benefits that flow from servant leadership efforts aimed at creating a community of faith that ministers to itself and to those within its reach.

The biblical methods of the servant work effectively in the contemporary church. The reason for the effectiveness of the servant model goes beyond the solid psychological and methodological principles that drive the model. Servant leadership works because it reflects the heart of the one who is both the Creator and the Redeemer of the human race. Leadership that bows to help others reflects the very nature of our Creator Savior. Servant leadership is an outflow of the Creator's own nature and an overflow of His redeeming love expressed within the context of leadership.

Recommendations for Further Study

An abundance of literature can be found for the pursuit of servant leadership studies. A major resource for pursuing servant studies is The Greenleaf Center for Servant Leadership, 921 East 86th Street, Indianapolis, IN, 46240. The center also hosts an excellent web site at www.greenleaf.org. A number of other related sites can be picked up from the Greenleaf site. A number of state universities support extensive servant leadership studies and research centers. These can be identified and located through the Greenleaf site.

The Greenleaf Center for Servant Leadership also sponsors an annual international conference for servant leadership, which is held at various venues throughout the country. *The Servant Leader* is a seasonal publication from the Greenleaf center. It offers locations of current servant leadership studies, practical helps, and suggested readings.

Two most helpful volumes that offer a wide range of topics on servanthood and servant leadership are *Insights on Leadership: Service, Stewardship, Spirit, and Servant-Leadership* and *Reflections on Leadership: How Robert K. Greenleaf's Theory of Servant Leadership Influenced Today's Top Management Thinkers,* both edited by Larry C. Spears. This project utilized both texts.

A number of other excellent texts are also recommended. Since boards control most group undertakings in the world, the work *The Unique Double Servant Leadership Role of the Board Chair Person,* by John Carver, could be helpful for a pastor endeavoring to gain new perspectives on issues of control, governance, and leading the church as a corporation. Carver sees the board as a venue for visible and powerful group servant leadership.

Greenleaf acted as a consultant for various religious organizations including seminaries and churches. His attitudes toward these organizations can be helpful for the individual needing an understanding of how institutional servanthood can relate to the church. "The Servant as Religious Leader" and "Seminary as Servant" are two excellent essays that endeavor to lead church related institutions into a higher awareness of servant opportunities in the world. Greenleaf argues that churches, acting as spiritually formative institutions, have an obligation and opportunity to nurture servants and *Spirituality as Leadership* may not look at spirituality in a classic evangelical perspective, but it offers Greenleaf's thoughts and arguments for churches acting as spiritually formative institutions that can more effectively influence and develop society as a caring entity.

A helpful and practical approach to journaling for servant leaders has been developed by Ann McGee-Cooper and Duane Trammell. *Awakening Personal and Team Genius: A Journaling Approach to Personal Growth and Servant Leadership* combines ideas, suggestions, and quotes of servanthood and servant leadership. The Robert K. Greenleaf Center for Servant-Leadership offers a catalog of resources for the asking.

Christian leaders must continually seek discovery of biblical expressions and notions of servanthood and servant leadership. The lives of Jesus, Paul, John, and Peter are excellent New Testament sources for discovering attitudes of servanthood that molded the lives of these great men and led them to challenge the Early Church to serve in the Spirit of Christ. A continuing research and application of key New Testament terms discussed in this project will prove an exciting and informative field of inquiry for the aspiring servant leader.

APPENDIX 1
INVITATION TO PARTICIPATE IN PROJECT

TRINITY BIBLE COLLEGE
50 South Sixth Avenue
Ellendale, North Dakota
58436-7150

DR. HOWARD L. YOUNG
President

701-349-3621
701-349-5443
(fax)

April 5, 2000

«Title» «FirstName» «LastName»
«Company»
«Address1»
«City», «State» «PostalCode»

Dear «Title» «LastName»:

Could you help me in a very important area of my personal and professional development? I am working on a Doctor of Ministry project that focuses on raising levels of Servant Leadership ministry through key leaders of the local church. I would like to invite you and, if married, your spouse to a special series of lectures on Servant-Leadership to be offered at the Glacier Bible Camp, beginning July 3, 2000. The series will be presented during the minister's hour during family camp There will be a one hour presentation each day. The lessons will be helpful, insightful and practical.

Even if you have no interest beyond the sessions at camp, you would find these sessions helpful. I am hopeful, however, that a number of pastors will join my research efforts. *But please do not feel that you will obligate yourself in any way if you attend.* You are welcome to attend and do nothing more than enjoy the time of teaching and sharing. I also encourage the attendance of any pastoral or church staff. More important than the research help you may give me, the development of servant leadership skills can be a pathway to church renewal and revitalization.

The research that follows the seminars is very simple and could be very helpful for your church. An inventory on servant leadership will be given (pretest) and the same survey will be given at the end of ninety days. During the interim period, you would be asked to plan and implement basic servant leadership strategies aimed at creating a higher sense of servant leadership in your church. These strategies can be as simple or as complicated as you want to make them. The seminar is intended to give you a vast array of options. It is proven that developing strategic servant leadership interventions contributes greatly to the spiritual formation of individuals involved, in many cases brings a sense of church revitalization, and often contributes to church growth.

Beyond the benefits listed above, those participating in the research will be given two credits from Trinity Bible College (nearly four hundred dollars worth of credit-free!) and a certificate of completion suitable for framing. The workbook for the course will also be free. The only homework will be implementing servant leadership strategies and measuring their success through a simple survey instrument. **Incidentally, the information gathered through the pre and post test is totally confidential.** I score the instrument and give the results to you as pastor. You may use the data anyway you wish. There is nothing about this project that should make you feel vulnerable. To the contrary, I believe the sessions and the strategic planning that follows the sessions could greatly benefit most churches.

If this seminar on leadership interests you on any level and you feel you might attend, please return the enclosed card indicating your interest. This information is needed as I plan for this leadership training.

I deeply appreciate Superintendent Goodman's invitation to make this a part of your summer family camp. Please send back your confirmation of interests for these sessions. A self addressed envelope is included for this purpose.

Sincerely,

Howard Young, President, Trinity Bible College

APPENDIX 2
RESPONSE TO INVITATION

Your invitation to a helpful and inspirational Servant-Leadership Institute. You will be given 2 college credits ($380.00 value) through Trinity Bible College. You will receive a seminar workbook and a certificate of completion.

Check one:

☐ Yes, I plan to attend and would consider participation in the study.

☐ Yes, I plan to attend but have no interest in the study.

Name ______________________________

Address ____________________________

Your invitation to a helpful and inspirational Servant-Leadership Institute. You will be given 2 college credits ($380.00 value) through Trinity Bible College. You will receive a seminar workbook and a certificate of completion.

Check one:

☐ Yes, I plan to attend and would consider participation in the study.

☐ Yes, I plan to attend but have no interest in the study.

Name ______________________________

Address ____________________________

APPENDIX 3
LIST OF ORIGINAL RESPONDENTS

NOT FORMALLY LISTED BECAUSE OF PRIVACY

APPENDIX 4
ORGANIZATIONAL LEADERSHIP ASSESSMENT (OLA)

INSTRUMENT NOT AVAILABLE

APPENDIX 5
CHART: ITEMS MEASURED BY THE OLA

CHART NOT AVAILABLE

APPENDIX 6
SERVANTHOOD STRATEGY GUIDELINES

Planning for Servant Leadership Strategies

Fundamental Questions:

1. *What is the duration of my plan?* Will it be short term, mid term, or long term in duration? For purposes of this study, a plan which anticipates a sixty to ninety day duration may be best. This does not, however, invalidate a plan that may run longer. You be the judge.

2. *What is the nature of the plan?* It may include one or more of the following basic approaches:

   Instructional approach: a series of teachings/sermons based upon the topic of servant leadership. It is strongly suggested that one or two nights of instruction in servant leadership be shared with first level servant leaders. This training should incorporate practical methods and solutions to everyday servant opportunities.

   Behavioral approach: Key servant leadership dedicates itself to observable servant leader behaviors and attitudes not already apparent in their kingdom service. These are personal behavioral changes that grow out of a personal examination of present behaviors and attitudes. For example, a pastor may feel the need to be more conversational or outwardly responsive to his congregants. Another individual might feel the need to be less defensive and give more attention to hearing and responding to the needs of others. This behavioral/attitudinal list may be as varied and long as it needs to be.
   A significant behavioral strategy could involve serving those on the first line level of the Servant's Stairway.

   The essential question: Can I foster and develop new attitudes and behaviors that better communicate a caring and sensitive servant leader ministry?

   Ministry approach: The context of servant leadership influence begins in the personhood of Christ and is experienced by those who are his undershepherds. At this point, the influence of servant leaders continues to escalate to a broader context until finally the church itself is a serving institution to its own, the community in which it exists, and the larger context of its world of limited influence, which could include regional, national, and international audiences.

   Servant programs could include both internal and external ministries. Internally, the church could design programs of ministry for the poor, single parents, those in crises of any kind, special needs individuals, and the elderly. What opportunities exist in the congregation? External programs could offer helps for the poor, homeless, unwedded mothers, prayer for government and city officials, bussing, community action groups, and many other opportunities.

3. *What are the most important components for successful planning?*

   Personal commitment-The pastor as servant leader is the key to developing other leaders and the church as servants to God and His people. You are called to set the example and make reasonable efforts to increase levels of servant leadership in the congregation. If you lead, people will follow.

Prayer-This may be the most important element of your servant leadership effort. The New Testament church literally changed the course of history, largely because first century Christians, including the apostles, saw their instrumentality in the kingdom through the eyes of servanthood. The fellowship of the Savior through prayer was a vital part of their spiritual journey. A prayerful discovery of the spirit and personality of Christ will lead to an humble and intentional ministry of service to the world around them (Matt.11:28-30).

Studies and Readings on Servanthood-Conducting a personal study of biblical passages related to servanthood will be helpful. Create your own scriptural bibliography on the topic of servanthood. Begin to build a library of servant texts. This research will lead to the development of sermons or lessons that can be foundational to your servanthood strategies at your present ministry post. Search the Internet. There are several resources out there. The Internet site for The Robert K. Greenleaf Center for Servanthood Studies is_______________________

Personal inventory of present pastoral habits and attitudes- Have recent church problems led you into a withdrawal from members of your congregation? A servant must at times be vulnerable. A willingness to engage the hurting and disenfranchised at personal risk is a characteristic of the true servant. Are there past experiences or personality traits that keep you from engaging members of your congregation on a servant level? Are you willing to allow the Holy Spirit to help you overcome personal obstacles or traits that keep you from going beyond your personal sense of pastoral duty?

Congregational inventory of needs-Query the congregation as to basic life needs that could be possibly addressed through a servant church. Defining the needs may take some time and will certainly take some amount of effort, but the outcome is worth it. A carefully planned questionnaire could be helpful. Personal observation and careful listening can also increase your awareness of the needs that a core of servant leaders could address.

Servant Leadership Awareness Strategies

The effective use of symbolism. Some churches still enact literal foot washing. Church leadership creating and signing a covenant of Servant Leadership which incorporates their servant commitment to the congregation.

A service recognizing the servant leaders within the church. Such a service could honor in any appropriate manner those who serve sacrificially.

Worship services that are designed around the theme of service to God, the church, and others. The sermon could also pick up on the theme and could incorporate simply commitment statements from those in the service.

The media of film and drama can be used effectively to promote servant leadership.
Utilize the bulletin board and the church bulletin to encourage servant attitudes and actions.

Public testimonials from effective servants and servant leaders. Allow others to inspire their fellows to accept the call of the servant.

Prayer efforts largely devoted to discovering and implementing the will of God for the development of a servant church.

Use church media to increase awareness for the need for servanthood. Congregational needs, servant opportunities, and testimonies could be a vital part of the church bulletin or monthly newsletter. Give servanthood all the "press" you can!

Write a servanthood tract or article and publish it for your people. People will follow your passion. Preach it, write it, sing it, pray it, and servants will discover a new way of looking at church and its ministries.

Strategizing for Servanthood

Name____

Church______________________________________

Address_____________________________________

The strongest strategies for a sixty or ninety day approach would involve a strong prayer component seeking God's will for servant ministries, a training component of first level servant leaders, and an applied strategy for developing first level servant leaders. Each of the strategies below should be specific in nature and include a time line or schedule for implementation.

A personal prayer strategy for developing pastoral servanthood:

APPENDIX 7

EVALUATION SHEET FOR SERVANT LEADERSHIP SEMINAR

Seminar Evaluation for Servant Leadership

Rate each question below on a scale of 1 to 5. If you strongly agree with the statement, a rating of 5 is appropriate. Lesser scores indicate less intense feelings about the statement.

Content

1. The content was well prepared. *Score:* ________
2. The content was relevant. *Score:* ________
3. The content was useful and practical. *Score:* ________
4. The content encouraged me to conduct further research on the topic. *Score:* ________
5. The content was biblically sound. *Score:* ________
6. The content gave me more hope and faith for my personal future. *Score:* ________
7. The content gave me more hope and faith for the future of my organization. *Score:* ________

Preparation

1. The instructor seemed well prepared. *Score:* ________
2. The instructor presented the material in an interesting manner. *Score:* ________
3. The content was clearly presented. *Score:* ________
4. The content was enthusiastically presented. *Score:* ________
5. The presentation was logically presented. *Score:* ________
6. The presentation was spiritually engaging. *Score:* ________
7. The presentation was intellectually engaging. *Score:* ________

Instructor

1. The instructor demonstrated a clear knowledge of the topic. *Score:* ________
2. The instructor had a professional appearance. *Score:* ________
3. The instructor demonstrated a caring attitude. *Score:* ________
4. The instructor endeavored to be helpful with the students. *Score:* ________
5. The instructor was friendly and open. *Score:* ________
6. The instructor seemed passionate about his topic. *Score:* ________
7. The instructor communicated the spirit and essence of his topic. *Score:* ________

APPENDIX 8
PASTORAL SERVANT LEADERSHIP QUESTIONAIRE

Pastoral Servant Leadership Questionnaire

Pastor ______________________________________
Church______________________________________

Do you feel your servant leadership project(s) significantly heightened your church's awareness of servanthood?

Do you feel your servant leadership project(s) significantly heightened your awareness of servanthood?

Do you feel more committed to personal servanthood since carrying out your project(s)?

Do you plan to continue developing and implementing servant strategies on a long-term basis?

Do you feel the servant project(s) benefited your church from a spiritual standpoint? In what ways?

Do you feel the servant project(s) benefited your church numerically?

Do you feel those leaders/individuals involved in the servant strategies have become stronger servants?

Please list three to five *personal* benefits this project(s) has provided.

Please list three to five *congregational* benefits this project(s) has provided.

List any future servant project(s) or strategies you are planning beyond the project?

Did the servant project(s) enable you to look at pastoral ministry any differently than before? If so, how?

Did the servant project(s) create any desire to continue researching the subject of servant leadership?

Will your personal development of servant leadership practices and qualities continue beyond the project(s)?

Circle the response that most accurately describes the results of your servant project(s).

There was little or no change in my congregation's attitude and response to servanthood efforts.

There was some change in my congregation's attitude and response to servanthood efforts.

There was significant positive change in my congregation's attitude and response to servanthood efforts.

Circle the most accurate response. As a result of my servant project(s), I believe the practice of servanthood in the church:

Probably has no impact upon church growth.

Has some impact on church growth.

Has significant positive impact upon church growth.

Circle the most accurate response. As a result of my servant project(s), I believe the practice of servanthood in the church:

Had little or no effect upon congregational spiritual life.

Had some effect upon congregational spiritual life.

Had significant positive effect upon congregational spiritual life.

Do you feel your servant strategies encouraged or fostered a sense of God's presence in worship services or other church functions?

Do you feel those who participated in your servant project(s) grew and developed in a manner that will continually enhance their service to others?

APPENDIX 9
LETTER TO ORIGINAL RESPONDENTS

TRINITY BIBLE COLLEGE
50 South Sixth Avenue
Ellendale, North Dakota
58436-7150

DR. HOWARD L. YOUNG
President

701-349-3621
701-349-5443
(fax)

May 1, 2000

Rev. D. Robin Storer
Cando Assembly of God
PO Box 398
Cando, ND 5832

Dear Rev. Storer:

I am delighted that you have indicated an interest in the Servant Leadership Seminar. Over the next few days, you will receive a Leadership Assessment Questionnaire (10 copies) that needs to be completed by yourself, any pastors on your staff, and board members up to ten people. If these two groups (board members, and/or other pastors) do not add up to 10 people, then other members of your congregation who are in voluntary leadership, or people who are actively involved in church activities should complete the questionnaire.

The questionnaire and its results will be held in strict privacy, but the overall results of the questionnaires will be a part of my studies. You will personally receive the results of the questionnaire and may use the data as you wish.

After the seminar--approximately three months later--you will be asked to have the same individuals complete the same questionnaire. This is what is called a pre-test--post-test configuration. When I send you the ten questionnaires, careful instructions will be given.

I wish to assure you of the high confidentiality of this process. I believe the study will provide for you very valuable insights and hopefully, along with the seminar, some quality help that can assist you in your leadership efforts. I pray you will find this process illuminating and personally, as well as congregationally, helpful.

Thank you again for being a part of this study. Other materials along with instructions will arrive over the next few days.

Sincerely,

Dr. Howard Young
President
Trinity Bible College

APPENDIX 10
LETTER ACCOMPANYING OLA

TRINITY BIBLE COLLEGE
50 South Sixth Avenue
Ellendale, North Dakota
58436-7150

DR. HOWARD L. YOUNG
President

701-349-3621
701-349-5443
(fax)

May 12, 2000

«Title» «FirstName» «LastName»
«Company»
«Address1»
«City», «State» «PostalCode»

Dear Rev. «LastName»:

Enclosed are ten questionnaires that will be a part of the study in which you have demonstrated an interest. These questionnaires are essentially an evaluation of the pastoral and administrative leadership of your church. Section one applies to the overall leadership team, including pastor(s), deacon board, and others who may take a vital role in leadership. Section Two, which addresses managers and top leadership, pertains to the pastor(s) of the church, including those who are voluntary or part time. Only those who work for the church in some capacity, particularly pastors, should fill out section three. Others who fill out the questionnaire may disregard it.

The ten questionnaires should be filled out by pastor(s) of the church and board members or advisory board members, and any other voluntary leadership in the church-Sunday School, Royal Rangers, Missionettes, Women's Ministries, etc. You may select the individuals involved. You may also use church members who are quite active and/or know well the leadership of the institution.

General Instructions are given on the questionnaire. Tell your people that their answers are confidential so they feel unencumbered when they complete the questionnaire. A postage paid envelope is attached to each questionnaire. After they have filled it out, they should mail it back to me. ***Encourage them to return the questionnaire within ten days. May I suggest you make a list of those who receive it and check them off as you discover they have returned it.***

Again, please stress to them the confidential nature of the questionnaire. You as a pastor will see only the total averages, not individual evaluations and you will see these only if you choose. I would recommend that you receive a report of averages from me, review it, and then decide whether the information can help you or not. You may share the overall information with the board and use the information to design a program of ministry through servant leadership strategies. This is my hope, but it will be solely up to you as pastor how you use the information. You may receive a copy of the complete study when it is finished about seven or eight months from now.

Additional steps for this process will be shared with you at the Servant Leadership Seminar. I am delighted you have shown an interest in participating in this study and training. I am praying that the seminar will be a blessing to you and ultimately to your church. Keep in mind that the effort put forth will be rewarded with two credit hours in leadership training from Trinity Bible College and a nice Leadership certificate suitable for framing.

These are opportune days for the church. I am thrilled with the prospects for kingdom expansion in every city, town, and community in America. The Servant Church can be excited about these precious days, which precede the coming of our Lord. Thank you for desiring to be faithful to the harvest! I look forward to seeing you at the seminar.

Sincerely,

Dr. Howard Young
President, Trinity Bible College

APPENDIX II
LETTER ENCOURAGING STRATEGY DEVELOPMENT

TRINITY BIBLE COLLEGE
50 South Sixth Avenue
Ellendale, North Dakota
58436-7150

June 13, 2000

DR. HOWARD L. YOUNG
President

701-349-3621
701-349-5443
(fax)

«Title» «FirstName» «LastName»
«Company»
«Address1»
«City», «State» «PostalCode»

Dear «Title» «LastName»:

It was a pleasure to have you in my recent session on Servant Leadership. I do hope the information was encouraging. Now that the seminar is completed, your development of a ninety-day "servant strategy" is a key factor in our work together. Keep in mind that the strategy should heavily involve your servant role toward key individuals in your church, particularly those who filled out or are in the process of filling out the questionnaire. Strategies involving the entire congregation are also desirable.

The main purpose of this correspondence is to let you know that I am happy to advise and assist you in any way I can. I am traveling frequently this summer, but you can leave a message with my secretary, Margaret. I speak with her daily when I'm out of the office. She will happily pass on any message in my absence. It would be a pleasure to assist you in any way. I am very excited about the possibilities of new ideas for servant leadership in our Dakota churches.

One more thing. If you would like to visit our campus and spend some time talking/strategizing servant leader methods, I would make myself available for a couple of hours in order to visit with you. If such a conference is desirable, call my secretary and give her possible dates for your visit. You may feel free to stay on campus if you need overnight accommodations. There would be no charge.

I have included a couple of things with this letter. A brief bibliography is included. I would encourage the purchase of two or three good texts on the topic of servant leadership. I have circled the books I feel would be most helpful to you. I have also enclosed a brief article devoted to Dr. Del Tarr at the time of his resignation at AGTS. He was truly a servant leader. If you haven't seen the article, I know it will be a blessing to you.

I am here to serve you. I want this effort of creating and implementing a plan to work well for you and your church. As I said in the seminar, this is not about one effort that will be carried out and forgotten. I believe a return to servant leadership is imperative if our churches are to flourish. Servant leadership is the basis of all that we do in our churches: prayer, soul winning, preaching and teaching, shepherd leadership and nurturing, and all the functions of a steward. Yes, it all flows from the servant heart.

Pray for my continued renewal as well. I am hungry for the Spirit of God to accomplish something new in my life. More than ever, I want to serve Christ and His church. I am pleased I can assist you. It is my prayer that I can be a blessing to you.

More later.

Your Servant,

Dr. Howard Young
President, Trinity Bible College

P.S. I am looking forward to receiving your servant leadership plan/strategy in the next few days.

APPENDIX 12
SECOND LETTER OF ENCOURAGEMENT

TRINITY BIBLE COLLEGE
50 South Sixth Avenue
Ellendale, North Dakota
58436-7150

DR. HOWARD L. YOUNG
President

701-349-3621
701-349-5443
(fax)

August 1, 2000

Rev. D. Robin Storer
Cando Assembly of God
PO Box 398
Cando, ND 58324

Dear Rev. Storer:

Greetings from the green prairies of North Dakota! I pray all is well in the good work that our Lord has given you. These are marvelous days to work in the vineyard of the Kingdom. I am deeply excited with the possibilities which lie before those with the zeal and determination to serve the Lord and His church with passion and gladness.

I know you are in the process of developing your strategy(s) for servant-leadership. I am standing with you in prayer as you follow through with this important aspect of future ministry. As I indicated in our recent seminar, I stand ready to help you in any manner. Please do not hesitate to call, write, or e-mail. My firm belief is that a program of servant-leadership can transform a local church. God's ideas and plans for serving the church are simply and unequivocally the best!

I wish to stay in touch with you and be of assistance. Your success has a deeper importance than my study. I am personally interested in your vision and work. You occupy a special place in the Kingdom and if I can help you move forward in your work, I am honored.

Stay in touch. Perhaps you could share a brief note on how things are going. My e-mail address is hyoung@drtel.net. My office phone is 701.349.5444 and my home phone is 701. 349.4078.

May God bless!

Servants Together,

Dr. Howard Young
President, Trinity Bible College

P.S. I have included a copy of a recent article on reaching secular people. This has been picked up by Enrichment and will be published in the future, but perhaps it can help you now.

APPRENDIX 13
LETTER PROVIDING ADDITIONAL TIME FOR STRATEGY IMPLEMENTATION

TRINITY BIBLE COLLEGE

50 South Sixth Avenue
Ellendale, North Dakota
58436-7150

DR. HOWARD L. YOUNG
President

701-349-3621
701-349-5443
(fax)

September 28, 2000

«Title» «FirstName» «LastName»
«Company»
«Address1»
«City», «State» «PostalCode»

Dear «Title» «LastName»:

Greetings from Trinity Bible College! I pray your servanthood strategies are going well. I have several emails from some of you and it appears that participation in the project has been a genuine blessing to you. *It is my prayer that your servant efforts will continue beyond this brief effort.* My greatest hope is that the Holy Spirit has done something very special in your life and the lives of those who have assisted you in this caring effort.

I still need two things from you. Please distribute the enclosed questionnaires to only those who filled out questionnaires in the beginning. Even if only two or three did questionnaires, it is important to get responses back from those same individuals. These need to be returned no later than November 15, 2000. I am putting data together now and these questionnaires form the heart of the project. Please note that this is a one month extension beyond what I asked for in my last correspondence. This will allow you one more full month to maintain your servant strategies and, hopefully, bring even a higher sense of servanthood leadership to your congregation.

If your servant strategies run their course by mid October, you may have the questionnaires returned at that time. If your strategy is completed by mid October, I would recommend another short term strategy of some nature for the period of mid October through mid November. *This is up to you. The longer the strategy or combination of strategies the greater the opportunity for influence upon your congregation. For this reason, if it is practical I would encourage a continuation or your present intervention or create a new short term intervention for about a thirty day period.*

I have included one new questionnaire for you as pastor. Your answers are extremely important to my final conclusions and observations about the project. I would like to get your questionnaire back by October 30. Please identify yourself and your church on the questionnaire. Add any comments you would like to make. You may send this questionnaire back by October 30, even if your church is still implementing a servant strategy.

I have included an article *Defining Servant Leadership* by Stan Plett. Many fine articles can be found on various sites on the internet. Some are much more detailed and better researched than others. A couple hours of browsing these sites can be helpful.

When things are wrapped up and data is compiled, I will send you the results as promised. Thank you for assisting me with this last stage of information gathering. **Please make every effort to get your respondents to return the questionnaires to me by November 15, 2000. I would advise you to give them the questionnaires about one week before the November due date.** This is critical to my work schedule.

God bless you. Thank you for being His servant!

Sincerely,

Howard Young
President, Trinity Bible College

APPRENDIX 14
LETTER FOR INTERPRETING COMPLETED ASSESSMENTS

Evangel Assembly of God

Pastor Howard Young

9920 W. Good Hope Road
Milwaukee, WI 53224

Phone: 414-353-6140
Fax: 414-353-0953
Email: PastorHYoung@aol.com

March 27, 2001

Dear Pastor,

Greetings from Milwaukee! I trust spring is well on its way in your part of the country. I have always enjoyed winter, but it does seem the older I get the more difficult it is to enjoy winter's claim.

Enclosed are the pretest and posttest scores for your servant leadership project. I have also included a summary of overall findings. This summary is a part of my doctoral project, so I send it to you for your personal evaluation of your servant leadership efforts. Please do not duplicate or distribute the original text that constitutes this report. You may copy any of the data you wish in a form helpful to you and distribute it to those who helped you with the study. Please also note that further recommendations are included.

Three sets of scores are included on your assessment summary. The ***first set*** is located in the upper right hand corner and records the numbers for the *three basic divisions* of the instrument. *Section one* of this set of scores measured servant leadership characteristics as they related to the entire organization. *Section two* measured servant leadership characteristics related to the leadership (you and your leadership team) of the organization. *Section three* measured the individuals completing the questionnaire and their individual perceptions of their role within the organization. The ***second and largest set*** of score is the middle section of the report and gives you your numbers for each of the sixty-six questions on the instrument. I have included a copy of the instrument in order that you may see the specific question along with its respective numbers. (Please do not copy the exam. It is protected by copyright.) The ***third set*** of scores is located in the lower left hand section of the instrument. It records scores for the six outstanding characteristics of servant oriented leadership measured by the instrument.

You will note that the three sets of scores gives the **pretest and posttest scores** and the difference between the two. Ideally, there will be a positive difference between the two numbers. Naturally, we hoped that the posttest scores would be higher than the pretest. The posttest scores represents the perception of your leadership after your servant leadership intervention(s) were in place for ninety to one hundred and twenty days.

As you read my general evaluations of the project, you will note that a majority of the churches participating enjoyed increases in many areas of the instrument. This was very encouraging to me, given the brief nature of training and intervention implementation. While this general increase in posttest scores is encouraging, it must be noted that the short duration of the intervention would not necessarily lend itself to a high degree of certainty about the data. Consequently, if your intervention did not produce a majority of positive numbers, please do not be discouraged.

I am greatly encouraged by the participation of your leadership in this study. *I encourage you to continually implement servant strategies in your church and exemplify the servant model within your church leadership, congregation, and community.* Servant leadership is the highest expression of authentic New Testament pastoral ministry and leadership. It ministers effectively within our churches because it is God's order for His church.

Your certificate of completion is included in this packet. You have also been given two hours of college credit with Trinity Bible College in Ellendale, North Dakota. Please express my deepest appreciation to those who assisted you in this study. I hope you take the time to share the enclosed data with them. My greatest desire is that this information will serve as a basis for developing more leadership and church strategies and interventions for the future.

I would be pleased to hear further news from you and your pastoral work. I remain ready to serve you as you endeavor to discover a new and exciting future for your pastoral work.

Blessings,

Howard Young

Pastor Howard Young

"...whoever wants to become great among you must be your servant..." — Matthew 20:26

APPENDIX 15
ASSESSMENT SHEET FOR PARTICIPATING CHURCHES

An Assessment of Pastoral Leadership in the Montana/North Dakota Districts of the Assemblies of God

Church: Calvary Assembly of God (Milbank, SD)
Pastor: Galen Rasmussen
Number of Questionnaires: Pre: 9 Post: 6
Respondent Profiles:

Pastor/Leadership:	Pre: 1	Post: 1
Board Member:	Pre: 4	Post: 2
Other:	Pre: 4	Post: 3

SET 1

	PRE	POST	DIFF
Section 1:	3.677	3.770	0.093
Section 2:	3.721	4.005	0.285
Section 3:	4.093	4.250	0.157

SET 2

	PRE	POST	DIFF		PRE	POST	DIFF
Question 1	4.222	4.000	-0.222	Question 34	3.889	4.167	0.278
Question 2	3.222	4.333	1.111	Question 35	3.889	4.000	0.111
Question 3	3.778	3.500	-0.278	Question 36	3.667	3.667	0.000
Question 4	3.889	4.167	0.278	Question 37	3.778	4.167	0.389
Question 5	2.889	3.833	0.944	Question 38	3.667	3.667	0.000
Question 6	3.889	4.000	0.111	Question 39	3.889	4.167	0.278
Question 7	4.000	3.500	-0.500	Question 40	3.778	4.167	0.389
Question 8	3.556	3.500	-0.056	Question 41	4.222	4.000	-0.222
Question 9	4.000	3.833	-0.167	Question 42	3.778	3.833	0.056
Question 10	4.222	4.000	-0.222	Question 43	3.222	3.333	0.111
Question 11	4.222	4.167	-0.056	Question 44	2.889	3.500	0.611
Question 12	3.778	3.667	-0.111	Question 45	3.333	3.667	0.333
Question 13	3.333	3.333	0.000	Question 46	4.111	4.167	0.056
Question 14	3.444	3.500	0.056	Question 47	4.222	4.000	-0.222
Question 15	3.556	3.333	-0.222	Question 48	4.000	4.000	0.000
Question 16	3.667	3.667	0.000	Question 49	3.444	4.000	0.556
Question 17	3.444	4.000	0.556	Question 50	3.222	3.500	0.278
Question 18	3.778	4.000	0.222	Question 51	3.556	4.167	0.611
Question 19	3.778	3.833	0.056	Question 52	3.556	4.167	0.611
Question 20	2.889	3.167	0.278	Question 53	3.667	4.333	0.667
Question 21	3.667	3.833	0.167	Question 54	3.556	4.167	0.611
Question 22	3.667	4.167	0.500	Question 55	4.444	4.333	-0.111
Question 23	3.778	4.167	0.389	Question 56	3.222	3.500	0.278
Question 24	4.111	4.167	0.056	Question 57	4.000	4.167	0.167
Question 25	4.222	4.167	-0.056	Question 58	4.333	4.167	-0.167
Question 26	3.222	3.833	0.611	Question 59	4.000	4.500	0.500
Question 27	3.889	4.000	0.111	Question 60	3.889	4.000	0.111
Question 28	3.889	4.333	0.444	Question 61	4.556	4.500	-0.056
Question 29	3.556	4.167	0.611	Question 62	4.444	4.667	0.222
Question 30	3.778	4.333	0.556	Question 63	4.111	4.333	0.222
Question 31	3.778	4.000	0.222	Question 64	3.667	4.000	0.333
Question 32	3.778	4.000	0.222	Question 65	4.333	4.500	0.167
Question 33	3.778	4.000	0.222	Question 66	4.111	4.333	0.222
	122.667	128.500	5.833		126.444	133.833	7.389
				score	3.774	3.975	0.200

SET 3

	PRE	POST	DIFF
Values People	3.825	3.960	0.135
Develops People	3.606	3.788	0.182
Builds Community	3.926	3.889	-0.037
Displays Authenticity	3.879	4.015	0.136
Provides Leadership	3.667	4.044	0.378
Shares Leadership	3.889	4.000	0.111

ABSTRACT

The majority of North Dakota and Montana Assemblies of God churches exist in rural environments and many of their leaders are desirous and/or needful of positive and transformational strategies that can assist local churches in providing an effective response to the following fundamental needs:

There is a need to create and implement a New Testament model of ministry that can effectively respond to various church cultures.

There is a need to develop a ministry model which helps dispel a growing perception of the church as narcissistic and self-serving.

There is a need for a model of ministry that equips and empowers both the professional ministry and laity for effective caring and support ministry in the church and in the community.

There is a need to provide a ministry in which low-trust toward leadership may be compounded by high-control leadership styles.

There is a need to create a caring ministry atmosphere, which enhances the possibility of local church revitalization.

The purpose, therefore, of the project is to develop an applied training seminar that will serve as a basis for the development of servant leadership attitudes and behaviors within pastors and lay leaders that respond to the preceding needs. Values inculcated into the seminar process encouraged the development of people through innovative and biblically based opportunities for personal growth, the building of community through specific strategies that incorporate collaborative work, the cultivation of personal authenticity by raising levels of integrity and trust, providing leadership by developing a compelling and visionary future, and sharing leadership by creating shared vision.

Following the seminar, a pretest and posttest configuration was implemented utilizing the Organizational Leadership Assessment (OLA). This sixty-six-item instrument was used to measure outstanding servant leadership characteristics before and after the application of prayerfully devised servant strategies in each participating local church. After the implementation of servant strategies in each church, a posttest was given with the intention of recognizing any positive trends initiated by the servant strategies. A general questionnaire was also utilized in order to assess individual pastor's perceptions of the value and significance of the applied effort.

Basic comparison of the pretest and posttest date took place at the end of the study. Qualitative and quantitative information was gathered and shared with each pastor and church at the end of the study.

SOURCES CONSULTED

Alexander, David, and Pat Alexander, eds. *Eerdman's Handbook to the Bible*. Herts, England: Lion Publishing, 1988.

Barclay, William. *New Testament Words: English New Testament Words Indexed with References to The Daily Study Bible*. Philadelphia: Westminster Press, 1974.

Barna, George. "Churches Lack Leadership: A Report by George Barna.", available from http://www.smartleadership.com/articles/churches.html; Internet accessed 30 August 2000.

__________. "The Second Coming of the Church, (A Blueprint for Survival) – Part Two."available from http://www.smartleadership.com/articles/churches.htlm. Internet accessed 30 August 2000.

Bass, B. M. *Stodgdill's Handbook of Leadership: A Survey of Theory and Research*. New York: The Free Press, 1981.

Bausch, Thomas A. *Insights on Leadership*. Edited by Larry Spears. New York: John Wiley & Sons, 1998.

Belleville, Linda, L. *Women Leaders and the Church: Three Crucial Questions*. Grand Rapids: Baker Books, 2000.

Bennis, Warren. *On Becoming a Leader*. Redding, Maine: Addison-Wesley Publishing, 1997.

Bethel, Sheila M. *Reflections on Leadership*. Edited by Larry Spears. New York: John Wiley & Sons, 1995.

Blanchard, Kenneth. *Insights on Leadership*. Edited by Larry Spears. New York: John Wiley & Sons, 1998.

Block, Peter. *Insights on Leadership*. Edited by Larry Spears. New York: John Wiley & Sons, 1998.

Blocker, Henri. *Songs of the Servant, Isaiah's Good News*. London: InterVarsity Press, 1975.

Booth, Wayne, Gregory Colomb, and Joseph Williams. *The Craft of Research*. Chicago: University of Chicago Press, 1995.

Borthwick, Paul. *A Mind for Missions: 10 Ways to Build Your World Vision*. Colorado Springs: NavPress, 1987.

Bouronnais, Gaetan. *Behold My Servant, Reading the Bible Thematically*. Minneapolis: Collegiate, 1974.

Briner, Bob. *Roaring Lambs: A Gentle Plan to Radically Change Your World*. Grand Rapids: Zondervan Publishing House, 1991.

Brody, Deborah. *Reflections on Leadership*. Edited by Larry Spears. New York: John Wiley & Sons, 1995.

Brown, L. David. *Take Care: A Guide for Responsible Living*. Minneapolis: Augsburg Publishing House, 1978.

Brox, Norbert. *Diakonia Churches for the Others*. Edinburgh: T and T Clark, 1988.

Bruce, Alexander Balmain. *The Training of the Twelve*. New York: Harper & Brothers Publishers, 1871.

Burns, James MacGregor. *Leadership*. New York: Harper & Row Publishers, 1979.

Butt, Howard E., Jr. *Renewing America's Soul: A Spiritual Psychology for Home, Work, and Nation.* New York: Continuum Publishing, 1996.

Cassidy, Richard J. *Jesus, Politics, and Society.* Maryknoll, N.Y.: Orbis Books, 1973.

Cedar, Paul A. *Strength in Servant Leadership.* Waco, Tex.: Word Books, 1987.

Cohen, A. R., S. L. Fink, and N. Josefowitz. *Effective Behavior in Organizations: Cases, Concepts, and Student Experiences.* Chicago: Irwin, 1995.

Cohen, William A. *The Art of the Leader.* Englewood Cliffs, N.J.: Prentice Hall, 1990.

Covey, Stephen R. *The 7 Habits of Highly Effective People.* New York: Simon & Schuster, 1989.

Crabb, Larry. *The Safest Place on Earth.* Nashville: Word Publishing, 1999.

Davis, Billie. *People, Tasks, & Goals.* Irving, Tex.: ICI University Press, 1997.

Delitzch, Fran. *Isaiah, vol. 7.* In *Commentary on the Old Testament in Ten Volumes.* Grand Rapids: William B. Eerdmans Publishing, 1982.

Dempster, Murray. *Called and Empowered: Global Mission in Pentecostal Perspective.* Edited by Bryon Klaus and Douglas Peterson. Peabody, Mass.: Hendrickson Publishers, 1991.

DePree, Max. *Leadership Is an Art.* New York: Dell Publishing, 1989.

Dinkmeyer, Don, and Daniel Eckstein. *Leadership by Encouragement.* Boca Raton, Fla.: St. Lucie Press, 1996.

Donahue, Bill. *Leading Life-Changing Small Groups.* Grand Rapids: Zondervan Publishing House, 1996.

Dudley, Carl S. *Making the Small Church Effective.* Nashville: Abingdon Press, 1978.

Eyres, Lawrence R. *The Elders of the Church.* Philadelphia: Presbyterian and Reformed Publishing, 1997.

Fenhagen, James C. *Invitation to Holiness.* San Francisco: Harper & Row, 1985.

Ford, Leighton. *Transforming Leadership: Jesus' Way of Creating Vision, Shaping Values and Empowering Change.* Downers Grove, Ill.: InterVarsity Press, 1991.

Fraker, Ann T. *Reflections on Leadership.* Edited by Larry Spears. New York: John Wiley & Sons, 1995.

Gaebelein, Frank, ed. *The Expositor's Bible Commentary,* vol. 6. Grand Rapids: Zondervan Publishing House, 1986.

Gardner, J. W. *Excellence.* New York: Harper & Brothers, 1984.

Getz, Gene, A. *Building Up One Another.* Wheaton, Ill.: Victor Books, 1979.

Greenleaf, Robert K. *On Becoming a Servant Leader.* San Francisco: Jossey-Bass Publishers, 1996.

_________. *The Power of Servant Leadership*. San Francisco: Berrett-Koehler Publications, 1998.

_________. *Servant Leadership*. Mahwah, N.J.: Paulist Press, 1977.

_________. *Servant Leadership: A Journey into the Nature of Legitimate Power and Greatness*. Mahwah, N.J.: Paulist Press, 1991.

Greenway, Roger, John Kyle, and Donald McGavran. *Missions Now: This Generation*. Grand Rapids: Baker Books, 1990.

Griffiths, Michael. *The Church and World Missions*. Grand Rapids: Zondervan Publishing House, 1982.

Guder, Darrell L., ed. *Missional Church: A Vision for the Sending of the Church in North America*. Grand Rapids: William B. Eerdmans Publishing, 1998.

Hall, Arlene S. *"Why a Great Leader."* In *Living Leadership: Biblical Leadership Speaks to Our Day*, ed. Kenneth Hall. Anderson, Ind.: Warner Press, 1991.

Hamner, W. Clay, and Dennis W. Organ. *Organizational Behavior: An Applied Psychological Approach*. Dallas: Business Publications, 1978.

Hedges, Charlie. *Getting the Right Things Right*. Sisters, Oreg.: Multnomah Books, 1996.

Heidebrecht, Vern. "Servant Leadership", [home page online]; available from http://www.mbconf.ca/mb/mbh3721/hern.html; Internet; accessed 21 August 2000.

Hesselbein, Frances, Marshall Goldsmith, and Richard Beckhard, eds. Druker Foundation. *The Leader of the Future.* San Francisco: Jossey-Bass Publishers, 1996.

Hocken, Peter. *The Glory and the Shame.* Guildford, Surrey: Eagle Publications, 1994.

Hofstede, Gert. *Cultures and Organizations, Software of the Mind.* New York: McGraw-Hill, 1997.

Horton, Michael Scott, ed. *Power Religion: The Selling Out of the Evangelical Church.* Chicago: Moody Press, 1992.

Horton, Stanley M. *Isaiah.* Springfield, Mo.: Logion Press, 1984.

Horvath, Terri. *Servant Leadership: An Old Idea Becomes New Again.* Available from http://www.cruise-in.com/resource/chrtser.html; Internet; accessed 21 August 2000.

Hunter, George G., III. *Church for the Unchurched.* Nashville: Abingdon Press, 1996.

Jones, Kenneth E. *The Weslyan Bible Commentary.* Vol. 3, *Isaiah-Malachi*. Grand Rapids: William B.Eerdmans Publishing, 1969.

Jones, E. Stanley. *The Way.* New York: Abingdon-Cokesbury Press, 1938

Kiechel, Walter, III. *Reflections on Leadership,* ed. Larry Spears. New York: John Wiley & Sons, 1995.

Kouzes, James M. and Barry Z. Posner. *Credibility.* San Francisco: Jossey-Bass Publishers, 1993.

__________. *Encouraging the Heart: A Leader's Guide to Rewarding and Recognizing Others.* San Francisco: Jossey-Bass Publishers, 1999.

_________. *The Leaders Challenge: How to Keep Getting Extraordinary Things Done in Organizations.* San Francisco: Jossey-Bass Publishers, 1999.

Ladd, George. *Perspectives on the World Christian Movement.* Edited by Ralph D. Winter and Steven C. Hawthorne. Pasadena, Calif.: William Carry Library, 1992.

Lassey, William R., ed. *Leadership and Social Change.* Iowa City, Iowa: University Associates Press, 1971.

Lee, Chris and Ron Zemke. *Reflections on Leadership*, ed. Larry Spears. New York: John Wiley & Sons, 1995.

Leupold, H.C. *Expositions of Isaiah.* Grand Rapids, Mich.: Baker Book House, 1983.

Lovelace, Richard F. *Dynamics of Spiritual Life: An Evangelical Theology of Renewal.* Downers Grove, Ill.: InterVarsity Press, 1990.

Luidens, Donald A. *Fighting Decline: Mainline Churches and the Tyranny of Aggregate Data.* The Christian Century, 6 November 1996.

Maxwell, John C. *Developing the Leader Within You.* Nashville: Thomas Nelson Publishers, 1993.

Maxwell, John C., and Jim Doran. *Becoming a Person of Influence.* Nashville: Thomas Nelson Publishers, 1997.

Millard, B. *Servant Leadership, It's Right and It Works!* Colorado Springs, Colo.: Life
Discovery Publications, 1995.

Miller, Calvin. *The Empowered Leader: Ten Keys to Servant Leadership*. Nashville: Broadman & Holman Publishers, 1995.

Murray, Andrew. *The Ministry of Intercessory Prayer.* Minneapolis: Bethany House, 1981.

Nanus, Burt. *Visionary Leadership*. San Francisco: Jossey-Bass Publishers, 1992.

Nouwen, Henri J. *In the Name of Jesus*. New York: Crossroad, 1989.

__________. *Reaching Out, The Three Movements of Spiritual Life*. New York: Doubleday, 1975.

North, C. R. *The Suffering Servant of God, Isaiah 40-55*. Bloomsbury Street, London: SCM Press, 1969.

Owens, R. G. *Organizational Behavior in Education*. Needham Heights: Allyn and Bacon, 1991.

Page, Don. *The Failure of the Christian Servant Leader.* Available from http://www/twu/ca/leadership/ch2-page.htmo; Internet; accessed 21 August 2000.

Parrish, Archie, and R. C. Sproul. *The Spirit of Revival: Discovering the Wisdom of Jonathan Edwards*. Wheaton, Ill.: Crossway Books, 2000.

Poling, James N., and Donald E. Miller. *Foundations for a Practical Theology of Ministry*. Nashville: Abingdon Press, 1985.

Rainer, Thomas S. *High Expectations*. Nashville: Broadman and Holman Publishers, 1999.

Richards, Lawerence O., and Clyde Hoeldtke. *A Theology of Church Leadership*. Grand Rapids: Zondervan Publishing House, 1980.

Rinehart, Stacy T. *Upside Down.* Colorado Springs: NavPress, 1998.

Roberts, J. *Servant Leaders: Beyond Hierarchy.* Self-published, 1996.

Rodenmayer, Robert N. *We Have This Ministry.* New York: Harper & Brothers Publishing, 1958.

Schwarz, Christian A. *Natural Church Development.* Carol Stream, Ill.: ChurchSmart Resources, 1996.

Senge, Peter M. *The Fifth Discipline.* New York: Doubleday, 1990.

Shawchuck, Norman. *What It Means to Be a Church Leader: A Biblical Point of View.* Leith, N. Dak.: Spiritual Growth Resources, 1984.

Shawchuck, Norman, and Roger Heuser. *Managing the Congregation: Building Effective Systems to Serve People.* Nashville: Abingdon Press, 1996.

Sider, Ron. *Perspectives on the World Christian Movement.* Edited by Ralph D. Winter and Steven C. Hawthorne. Pasadena, Calif.: William Carey Library, 1992.

Sims, B. J. *Servanthood: Leadership for the Third Millennium.* Boston: Cowley Publications, 1997.

Snyder, Howard, A. *A Kingdom Manifesto: Calling the Church to Live Under God's Reign.* Downers Grove, Ill.: InterVarsity Press, 1985.

_________. *Models of the Kingdom.* Nashville: Abingdon Press, 1991.

_________. *Signs of the Spirit*. Downers Grove, Ill.: InterVarsity Press, 1991.

_________. *The Community of the King*. Downers Grove, Ill.: InterVarsity Press, 1971.

Spears, Larry C., ed. *Insights on Leadership: Service, Stewarship, Spirit, and Servant-Leadership*. New York: John Wiley & Sons, 1998.

_________. *Reflections on Leadership*. New York: John Wiley & Sons, 1995.

Spence, H. D. M. and Joseph S. Exell, eds. *The Pulpit Commentary*. Vol. 10, *Isaiah*. Grand Rapids: William B. Eerdmans Publishing, 1980.

Steers, Richard and Lyman Porter. *Motivation and Work Behavior*. New York: McGraw-Hill, 1983.

Stogdill, Ralph M. *Handbook of Leadership*. New York: The Free Press, 1974.

Tatum, James B. *Reflections on Leadership*, Edited by Larry Spears. New York: John Wiley & Sons, 1995.

Turner, William B. *A Journey toward Servant Leadership*. Macon, Ga.: Smyth & Helwys Publishing, 2000.

Vine, W. E. *Vine's Expository Dictionary of Old and New Testament Words*. Old Tappan: Fleming H. Revell, 1981.

Wagner, Peter C. *Leading Your Church into Growth: The Secret of Pastor/People Partnership in Dynamic Church Growth*. Ventura, Calif.: Regal Books, 1984.

Walvoord, John F., and Roy B. Zuck, eds. *The Bible Knowledge Commentary: An Exposition of Scriptures by Dallas Theological Seminary Faculty.* Wheaton, Ill.: Victor Books, 1978.

Weatherhead, Leslie D. *In Quest of a Kingdom: A Challenging Interpretation of the Gospel.* Nashville: Abingdon Press, 1944.

White, James E. *Rethinking the Church.* Grand Rapids: Baker Books, 1997.

Wong, Paul T. P. *The Challenge of Open Leadership.* Available at http://www.twu.ca/cpsy/faculty/wong/leadership/openleader.html; Internet; accessed 21 August 2000.

York, John. *Missions in the Age of the Spirit.* Springfield, Mo.: Logion Press, 2000.

Young, David S. *Servant Leadership for Church Renewal.* Scottsdale, Pa.: Herald Press, 1999.

Endnotes

1 George Barna, "Churches Lack Leadership: A Report by George Barna" [home page on-line]; available from http://www.smartleadership.com/articles/churches.html; Internet; accessed 30 August 2000.

2 Peter Hocken, *The Glory and the Shame* (Guildford, Surrey: Eagle Publications, 1994), 14.

3 Paul T.P. Wong, "The Challenge of Open Leadership" [home page on-line]; available from http://www.twu.ca/cpsy/faculty/wong/leadership/openleader.html, Internet; accessed 21 August 2000.

4 Ibid.

5 Ibid.

6 Terri Horvath, "Servant Leadership: An Old Idea Becomes New Again" [home page on-line]; available from http://www.cruise-in.com/resource/chrtser.html; Internet; accessed 21 August 2000.

7 Don Page, "The Failure of the Christian Servant Leader" [home page on-line]; available from http://www.twu.ca/leadership/ch2-page.html; Internet; accessed 21 August 2000.

8 Phil. 2:3-7. All scripture quotations, unless otherwise noted, are from the New International Version.

9 Page, "The Failure of the Christian Servant Leader."

10 George Barna, "The Second Coming of the Church (A Blueprint for Survival)–Part Two" [on line Manna home page]; available from http://www.wolc.org/manna/february/blueprint.html; Internet; accessed 30 August 2000.

11 Ibid.

12 Donald A. Luidens, "Fighting Decline: Mainline Churches and the Tyranny of Aggregate Data," *The Christian Century*, 6 November 1996, 19.

13 Ibid.

14 Larry C. Spears, ed., *Reflections on Leadership* (New York: John Wiley & Sons, 1995), 129.

15 Ibid, 143.

16 Gaetan Bourbonnais, *Behold My Servant, Reading the Bible Thematically* (Minneapolis: Collegiate, 1974), 15.

17 Ibid.

18 Exod. 3:12.

19 Cf. Exod. 4:23 (serve); 5:1 (keep a feast); 5:3, 8, 17 (sacrifice); 8:21, 23, 24, 25 (sacrifice); 9:1, 13 (serve); 10:3, 7, 8 (serve); 10:9 (a feast of Yahweh); 10:11, 24, 26 (serve); in verse 25 (sacrifices and holocausts); 12:31 (serve).

20 Exod. 32:31-32.

21 First Sam. 12:5.

22 Kenneth E. Jones, *The Weslyan Bible Commentary*, vol.3, *Isaiah-Malachi* (Grand Rapids: Eerdman's Publishing, 1969), 136.

23 Peter's preaching on the Day of Pentecost (Acts 2:22-40) conveyed a clear understanding that the sufferings of the Savior were an essential part of the process that would eventually lead Christ to the Throne of David, there to reign as King of the New Kingdom. In this position, He would pour forth the Spirit that becomes the uniting and empowering force behind God's kingdom on earth.

24 Frank Gaebelein, ed., *The Expositors Bible Commentary*, vol.6 (Grand Rapids: Zondervan, 1986), 300.

25 John F. Walvoord and Roy B. Zuck, eds., *The Bible Knowledge Commentary: An Exposition of the Scriptures by Dallas Seminary Faculty* (Wheaton, Ill.: Victor Books, 1978), 1107-8.

26 C. R. North, *The Suffering Servant of God, Isaiah 40-55* (London: SCM Press, 1969), 30.

27 Peter explained that the God of the patriarchs (themselves *servants* of God) glorified *His servant Jesus* through resurrection from the dead. This qualifies Him to be the Righteous One and the Author of life (Acts 3:13-15).

28 Henri Blocker, *Songs of the Servant, Isaiah's Good News* (London: InterVarsity Press, 1975), 11.

29 See Gal. 4:26-27. Referencing the spiritual children of Abraham, this passage ties the ultimate children of the Servant's kingdom to the children of the New Jerusalem in heaven. The children of Abraham will be as numerous as the individuals coming under the influence (tent) of the Servant (Isa. 54:3).

30 Stanley M. Horton, *Isaiah* (Springfield, Mo.: Logion Press, 1984), 396-7.

31 H. C. Leupold, *Exposition of Isaiah* (Grand Rapids.: Baker Book House, 1983), 236-46.

32 Fran Delitzch, *Isaiah*, in *Commentary on the Old Testament in Ten Volumes*, vol. 7 (Grand Rapids: Eerdmans Publishing, 1982).

33 Mark 10:45, KJV.

34 Jesus told His disciples, "As my Father has sent me, even so I send you" (John 20:21, KJV). It seems certain that the disciples would have understood this commissioning to witnessing and evangelism and the need to incorporate the self-denying and servant attitude that constantly characterized His ministry to the world around them and leadership among them.

35 Luke 4:18-19.

36 Leupold, Exposition of Isaiah, 320.

37 H. D. M. Spence and Joseph S. Exell, eds., *The Pulpit Commentary*, vol.10, Isaiah, (Grand Rapids: Eerdmans Publishing), 414-15.

38 Larry C. Spears, ed., *Insights on Leadership: Service, Stewardship, Spirit, and Servant-Leadership* (New York: John Wiley & Sons, Inc., 1998), 27.

39 Leighton Ford, *Transforming Leadership: Jesus' Way of Creating Vision, Shaping Values and Empowering Change* (Downers Grove, Ill.: InterVarsity Press, 1991), 148.

40 Matt. 20:25-28.

41 Lawrence O. Richards and Clyde Hoeldtke, *A Theology of Church Leadership* (Grand Rapids: Zondervan, 1980), 106-7.

42 Ford, 150.

43 Donald E. Miller and James N. Poling, *Foundations for a Practical Theology of Ministry* (Nashville: Abingdon Press, 1985), 20.

44 Ibid., 21.

45 John 13:14-17.

46 Stacy T. Rinehart, *Upside Down* (Colorado Springs, Colo.: Navpress, 1998), 72.

47 Ibid., 76.

48 Eph. 2:19, 22.

49 Rhinehart, *Upside Down,* 75.

50 First Pet. 4:10.

51 Paul A. Cedar, *Strength in Servant Leadership* (Waco, Tex.: Word Books, 1987), 62-63.

52 Eph. 4:11-12.

53 L. David Brown, *Take Care: A Guide for Responsible Living* (Minneapolis: Augsburg Publishing House, 1978), 100.

54 William Barclay, *New Testament Words: English New Testament Words Indexed with References to The Daily Study Bible* (Philadelphia: Westminster Press, 1974), 177-78.

55 Brown, 110.

56 George Ladd, *Perspectives on the World Christian Movement,* eds. Ralph D. Winter and Steven C. Hawthorne (Pasadena, Calif.: William Carry Library, 1992), A66-A67.

57 Howard Synder, *Models of the Kingdom* (Nashville: Abingdon Press, 1991), 83-84.

58 Ron Sider, *Perspectives on the World Christian Movement,* eds. Ralph D. Winter and Steven C. Hawthorne (Pasadena, Calif.: William Carey Library, 1992), A86-A87.

59 Ibid., A85.

60 Howard A. Snyder, *The Community of the King* (Downers Grove, Ill.: InterVarsity Press, 1971), 107-115.

61 Ibid.,114-15.

62 Snyder offers a five dimensional approach to church renewal. These dimensions include personal, corporate, conceptual, structural, and missiological renewal. He contends that the latter is imperative for full and meaningful spiritual renewal. A church has not really been renewed until it has found its unique mission for God's kingdom in the here and now. (Howard Snyder, *Signs of the Spirit* (InterVarsity Press, 1991), Chapter 8.

63 Rhinehart, 88.

64 Ibid., 89-90.

65 Richards and Hoeldtke, 92.

66 Robert K. Greenleaf, *Servant Leadership: A Journey into the Nature of Legitmate Power and Greatness* (Mahwah, N.J.: Paulist Press, 1991), 81.

67 Ibid.

68 Ibid., 61.

69 C. Peter Wagner, *Leading Your Church to Growth: The Secret of Pastor/People Partnership in Dynamic Church Growth* (Ventura, Calif.: Regal Books, 1984), 108.

70 Michael Griffiths, *The Church and World Missions* (Grand Rapids: Zondervan, 1982), 63.

71 Darrell L. Guder, ed., *Missional Church: A Vision for the Sending of the Church in North America* (Grand Rapids: Eerdmans Publishing, 1998), 223.

72 Ibid., 148.

73 Ibid.

74 David Alexander and Pat Alexander, eds., *Eerdmans' Handbook to the Bible* (Herts, England: Lion Publishing, 1988), 88.

75 Calvin Miller, *The Empowered Leader: Ten Keys to Servant Leadership* (Nashville: Broadman & Holman Publishers, 1995), 200-201.

76 W. E. Vine, *Vine's Expository Dictionary of Old and New Testament Words* (Old Tappen, N.J.: Fleming H. Revell, 1981), 744.

77 Norman Shawchuck and Roger Heuser, *Managing the Congregation: Building Effective Systems to Serve People,* (Nashville: Abingdon Press, 1996), 21.

78 Lawrence R. Eyres, *The Elders of the Church,* (Philadelphia: Presbyterian and Reformed Publishing, 1975), 59-69.

79 Synder, *The Community of the King,* 82-84.

80 Synder's *The Community of the King* provides an excellent resource for those endeavoring to build a ministering church that expresses itself through a functional and compassionate church culture. Snyder's understanding of the functionality of New Testament leadership and the emerging kingdom of God within the church is helpful for those desiring a more complete understanding of the church as Kingdom under God's reign.

81 Luke 22:24-27. Jesus points leadership in the direction of humility and service which would require extensive changes in the way that His disciples viewed future service in His kingdom. Under the influence of the Holy Spirit, His disciples were to be the architects of His new order on earth. They

could not look toward patterns in the world any more than contemporary leaders can take their cue from the world around them.

82 Matt. 22:1-14, "Go to the street corners and invite anyone you can find" is not as much a statement of desperation to fill the wedding hall as it is a statement of God's love and acceptance of individuals who need a sense of belonging to His kingdom.

83 Luke 14:7-11. Servants of the Kingdom are possessed with a deep humility. Pride can lead to positioning, which meets with Jesus' deep disapproval.

84 Richard J. Cassidy, *Jesus, Politics, and Society* (Maryknoll, N.Y.: Orbis Books, 1971), 37-40.

85 Luke 17:7-10. This may be Jesus' most explicit statement on the dedication of hardworking servants. Servants do not question the difficulty of the task, the urgency of the master, or the propriety or order of the estate, for no other reason than the fact that they are mere servants.

86 James C. Fenhagen, *Invitation to Holiness* (San Francisco: Harper and Row, 1985), 71-72.

87 Norbert Brox, *Diakonia Churches for the Others* (Edinburgh: T and T Clark, 1988), 33.

88 Ibid., 35.

89 Jesus promised that He would build His church (Matt.16:17-18). Logically, the Book of Acts became a focal point as to the methods and means by which this promise was accomplished. Consequently, the contemporary church is benefited greatly by a close examination and reproduction of the attitudes, qualities, and driving philosophies of ministry by which the first-century church gained a foothold in a pagan environment.

90 Snyder, *Models of the Kingdom*, 23, 147.

91 Ralph M. Stogdill, *Handbook of Leadership* (New York: The Free Press, 1974), 7.

92 James MacGregor Burns, *Leadership* (New York: Harper & Row, 1979), 19.

93 William A. Cohen, *The Art of the Leader* (Englewood Cliffs, N.J.: Prentice Hall, 1990), 3.

94 John C. Maxwell, *Developing the Leader within You* (Nashville: Thomas Nelson Publishers, 1993), 1.

95 A. R. Cohen, S. L. Fink, and N. Josefowitz, *Effective Behavior in Organizations: Cases, Concepts, and Student Experiences* (Chicago: Irwin Company, 1995), 30.

96 Warren Bennis, *On Becoming A Leader* (Redding, Maine: Addison-Wesley Publishing, 1997), 39-42.

97 Leighton Ford, *Transforming Leadership: Jesus' Way of Creating vision, Shaping Values and Empowering Change (Downers Grove, Ill.: InterVarsity Press, 1991),* 26-27.

98 B. M. Bass, *Stodgdill's Handbook of Leadership: A Survey of Theory and Research* (New York, 1981), chapters 1 and 2.

99 Larry C. Spears, ed., *Reflections on Leadership* (New York: John Wiley & Sons, 1995), 2.

100 Max DePree, *Leadership Is an Art* (New York: Dell Publishing, 1989), 12.

101 Norman Shawchuck and Roger Heuser, *Managing the Congregation: Building Effective Systems to Serve People*, (Nashville: Abingdon Press, 1996), 183.

102 Peter Block, *Insights on Leadership*, ed. Larry Spears (New York: John Wiley & Sons, 1998), 5.

103 Chris Lee and Ron Zemke, *Reflections on Leadership*, ed. Larry Spears (New York: John Wiley & Sons, 1995), 102-103.

104 James B. Tatum, *Reflections on Leadership*, ed. Larry Spears (New York: John Wiley & Sons, 1995), 308.

105 Gert Hofstede, *Cultures and Organizations, Software of the Mind* (New York: McGraw-Hill, 1997), 28, 141.

106 Spears, *Reflections on Leadership*, 3.

107 Robert K. Greenleaf, *Servant Leadership* (Mahwah, N.J.: Paulist Press, 1977), 13.

108 Robert K. Greenleaf, *Servant Leadership: A Journey into the Nature of Legitimate Power and Greatness* (Mahwah, N.J.: Paulist Press, 1991), 66-67.

109 Robert K. Greenleaf, *The Power of Servant Leadership* (San Francisco: Berrett-Koehler Publications, 1998), 61.

110 Greenleaf, *Servant Leadership*, 10.

111 Ibid., 4.

112 Ibid., 10.

113 Don Page, "The Failure of the Christian Servant Leader" [home page on-line]; available from http://www.twu.ca/leadership/ch2-page.html; Internet; accessed 21 August 2000.

114 Ibid., 16.

115 Lee and Zemke, 100.

116 Greenleaf, *Servant Leadership*, 68.

117 Ibid., 110.

118 Arlene S. Hall, "Why a Great Leader," in *Living Leadership: Biblical Leadership Speaks To Our Day* (Anderson, IND.: Warner Press, 1991), 14.

119 R. G. Owens, *Organizational Behavior in Education* (Needham Heights, Mass.: Allyn and Bacon, 1991), 26.

120 Paul A. Cedar, *Strength in Servant Leadership* (Waco, Tex.: Word Books, 1987), 65.

121 Sheila M. Bethel, *Reflections on Leadership*, ed. Larry Spears (New York: John Wiley & Sons, 1995), 19.

122 Thomas S. Rainer, *High Expectations* (Nashville: Broadman & Holman Publishers, 1999), 70-71.

123 Greenleaf, *Servant Leadership*, 246-48.

124 Darrell L. Guder, ed., *Missional Church: A Vision for the Sending of the Church in North America* (Grand Rapids: Eerdmans Publishing, 1998), 148.

125 Gene A. Getz, *Building Up One Another* (Wheaton, Ill.: Victor Books, 1979), 5.

126 James N. Poling and Donald E. Miller, *Foundations for a Practical Theology of Ministry* (Nashville: Abingdon Press, 1985), 165.

127 Robert N. Rodenmayer, *We Have this Ministry* (New York: Harper & Brothers, 1958), 116.

128 Richard F. Lovelace, *Dynamics of Spiritual Life: An Evangelical-Theology of Renewal* (Downers Grove, Ill.: InterVarsity Press, 1990), 389.

129 Roger Greenway, John Kyle, and Donald McGarvan, *Missions Now: This Generation* (Grand Rapids: Baker Book House, 1990), 120.

130 Paul Borthwick, *A Mind For Missions: 10 Ways to Build Your World Vision* (Colorado Springs: Navpress, 1987), 135.

131 John York, *Missions in the Age of the Spirit* (Springfield, Mo.: Logion Press, 2000), 58.

132 Guder, 105.

133 Henri J. Nouwen, *In the Name of Jesus* (New York: Crossroad, 1989), 93.

134 Alexander Balmain Bruce, *The Training of the Twelve* (New York: Harper & Brothers Publishers, 1871), 524.

135 Lee and Zemke, 101.

136 Thomas A. Bausch, *Insights on Leadership*, ed. Larry Spears (New York: John Wiley & Sons, 1998), 241.

137 B. J. Sims, *Servanthood: Leadership for the Third Millennium* (Boston: Cowley Publications, 1997), 10-11.

138 Ibid., 18.

139 J. W. Gardner, *Excellence* (New York: Harper and Brothers, 1984), 152.

140 Ibid., 22.

141 Ann T. Fraker, *Reflections on Leadership*, ed. Larry Spears (New York: John Wiley & Sons, 1995), 46.

142 Greenleaf, *Servant Leadership*, 10.
143 Charlie Hedges, *Getting the Right Things Right* (Sisters, Oreg.: Multnomah Books, 1996), 188.
144 William A. Cohen, *The Art of the Leader* (Englewood Cliffs, N.J.: Prentice Hall, 1990), 139-40.
145 Don Dinkmeyer and Daniel Eckstein, *Leadership By Encouragement* (Boca Raton, Fla.: St. Lucie Press, 1996), 197.
146 James M. Kouzes and Barry Z. Posner, *Credibility* (San Francisco: Jossey-Bass Publishers, 1993), 71.
147 James E. White, *Rethinking the Church* (Grand Rapids: Baker Book House, 1997), 74.
148 Spears, *Reflections on Leadership*, 2.
149 Vern Heidebrecht, "Servant Leadership", [home page online]; available from http://www.mbconf.ca/mb/mbh3721/hern.html; Internet; accessed 21 August 2000.
150 B. Millard, *Servant Leadership: It's Right and It Works!* (Colorado Springs, Colo.: Life Discovery Publications, 1995), 3.
151 Ibid.
152 Ibid.
153 Norman Shawchuck, *What it Means to Be a Church Leader: A Biblical Point of View* (Leith, N. Dak.: Spiritual Growth Resources, 1984), 14-15.
154 Stacy T. Rinehart, *Upside Down* (Colorado Springs: NavPress, 1998), 9.
155 Burns, *Leadership*, 248-49.
156 Billie Davis, *People, Tasks, and Goals* (Irving, Tex.: ICI University Press, 1997), 199.
157 Bill Donahue, *Leading Life-Changing Small Groups* (Grand Rapids: Zondervan, 1996), 37-38.
158 Bob Briner, *Roaring Lambs: A Gentle Plan to Radically Change Your World* (Grand Rapids: Zondervan, 1991), 47.
159 Walter Kiechel III, *Reflections on Leadership*, ed. Larry Spears (New York: John Wiley & Sons, 1995), 122-23.

160 J. Roberts, *Servant Leaders: Beyond Hierarchy* (Self-Published), 54.

161 Lawrence O. Richards and Clyde Hoeldtke, *A Theology of Church Leadership* (Grand Rapids: Zondervan, 1980), 298.

162 David L. Brown, *Take Care: A Guide for Responsible Living* (Minneapolis: Augsburg Publishing House, 1978), 109.

163 Ibid., 28-30.

164 Henri J. Nouwen, 62-63.

165 Kouzes and Posner, 15.

166 Ibid., 165.

167 Ibid., 167, 81.

168 Robert K. Greenleaf, *On Becoming a Servant Leader* (San Francisco: Jossey-Bass Publishers, 1996), 154-56.

169 Peter C. Wagner, *Leading Your Church into Growth: The Secret of Pastor/People Partnership in Dynamic Church Growth* (Ventura, Calif.: Regal Books, 1984), 86.

170 Richards and Hoeldtke, 44.

171 Burt Nanus, *Visionary Leadership* (San Francisco: Jossey-Bass Publishers, 1992), 159.

172 Peter M. Senge, *The Fifth Discipline* (New York: Doubleday, 1990), 4.

173 Frances Hesselbein, Marshall Goldsmith, and Richard Beckhard, eds., *The Leader of the Future* (San Francisco: Jossey-Bass Publishers, 1996), 242-46.

174 Christian A. Schwarz, *Natural Church Development* (Carol Stream, Ill.: ChurchSmart Resources, 1996), 32.

175 William B. Turner, *A Journey toward Servant Leadership* (Macon, Ga.: Smyth & Helwys Publishing, 2000), 152.

176 Howard E. Butt Jr., *Renewing America's Soul: A Spiritual Psychology for Home, Work, and Nation* (New York: Continuum Publishing, 1996), 88.

177 Howard A. Snyder, *A Kingdom Manifesto: Calling the Church to Live under God's Reign* (Downers Grove, Ill.: InterVarsity Press, 1985), 111-20.

178 Leslie D. Weatherhead, *In Quest of a Kingdom: A Challenging Interpretation of the Gospel* (Nashville: Abingdon Press, 1944), 148.

179 David S. Young, *Servant Leadership for Church Renewal* (Scottsdale, Pa.: Herald Press, 1999), 77.

180 Nouwen, 62-64.

181 Archie Parrish and R. C. Sproul, *The Spirit of Revival: Discovering the Wisdom of Jonathan Edwards* (Wheaton, Ill.: Crossway Books, 2000), 170.

182 George G. Hunter III, *Church for the Unchurched* (Nashville: Abingdon Press, 1996), 144.

183 Murray Dempster, *Called and Empowered: Global Mission in Pentecostal Perspective*, eds. Bryon Klaus and Douglas Peterson (Peabody, Mass.: Hendrickson Publishers, 1991), 32-38.

184 Nouwen, 219-20.

185 Calvin Miller, *The Empowered Leader: Ten Keys to Servant Leadership* (Nashville: Broadman & Holman Publishers, 1995), 53-54.

186 Larry Crabb, *The Safest Place on Earth* (Nashville: Word Publishing, 1999), 19.

187 Shawchuck, 14.

188 Larry C. Spears, ed., *Reflections on Leadership* (New York: John Wiley & Sons, 1998), 4.

189 Ibid., 76-78.

Made in the USA
Monee, IL
13 January 2023

25212059R00114